JUMBLE® Cuisine

Puzzles to Savor!

Henri Arnold,
Bob Lee,
Jeff Knurek, &
David L. Hoyt

TRIUMPH BOOKS

This book is available in quantity at special discounts
for your group or organization.

For further information, contact:
Triumph Books LLC
814 North Franklin Street
Chicago, Illinois 60610
Phone: (312) 337-0747
www.triumphbooks.com

Printed in U.S.A.
ISBN: 978-1-62937-735-3

Design by Sue Knopf

Contents

JUMBLE®
Cuisine

Classic Puzzles

PUZZLE

1

JUMBLE®

Unscramble these four Jumbles, one letter to each square, to form four ordinary words.

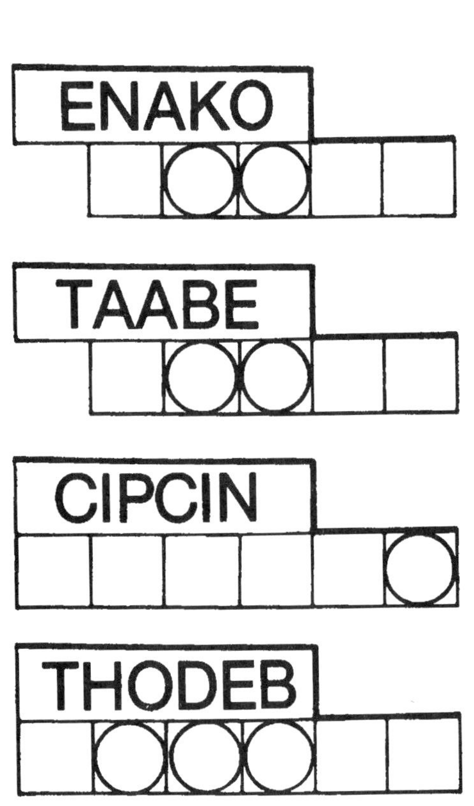

Now arrange the circled letters to form the surprise answer, as suggested by the above cartoon.

Print answer here AT THE ◯◯◯◯ OF THE ◯◯◯◯

JUMBLE®

Unscramble these four Jumbles, one letter to each square, to form four ordinary words.

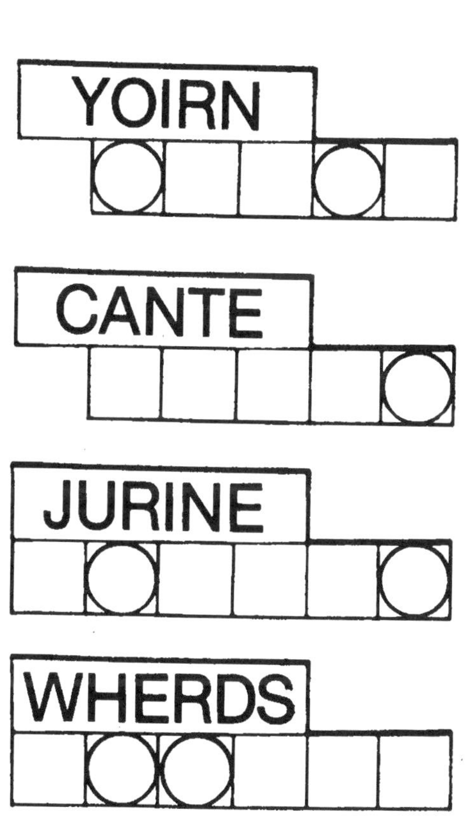

Now arrange the circled letters to form the surprise answer, as suggested by the above cartoon.

Print answer here “  ”

JUMBLE®

Unscramble these four Jumbles, one letter to each square, to form four ordinary words.

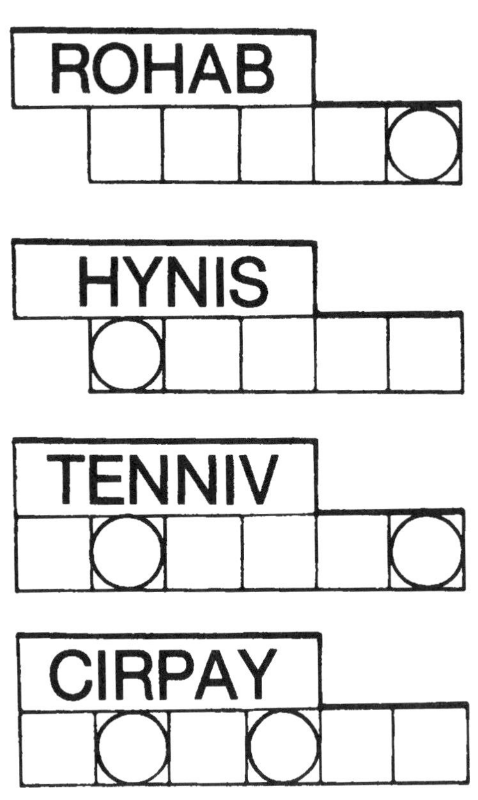

Now arrange the circled letters to form the surprise answer, as suggested by the above cartoon.

Print answer here " "

PUZZLE

4

JUMBLE®

Unscramble these four Jumbles, one letter to each square, to form four ordinary words.

KECHO
POSOW
REMPIT
ENGOUT
You've had enough!
WHAT A MAN WHO DRINKS TO FORGET OFTEN FORGETS.

Now arrange the circled letters to form the surprise answer, as suggested by the above cartoon.

Print answer here ◯◯◯◯ TO ◯◯◯◯

JUMBLE®

Unscramble these four Jumbles, one letter to each square, to form four ordinary words.

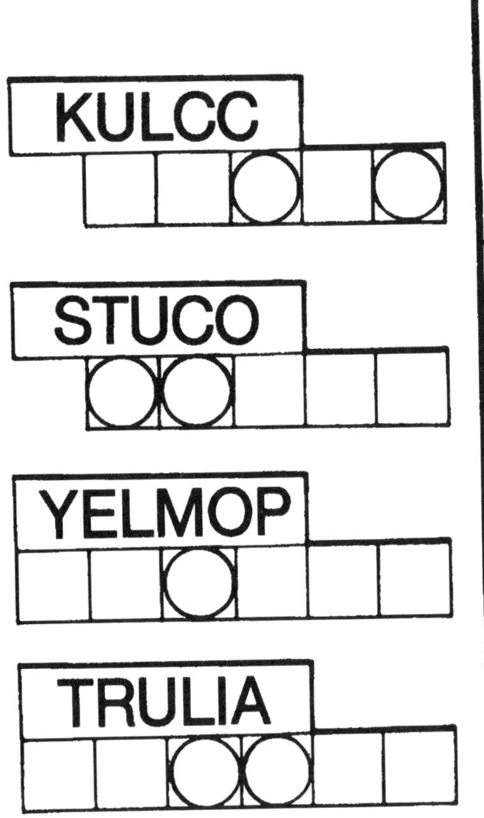

Now arrange the circled letters to form the surprise answer, as suggested by the above cartoon.

Print answer here

PUZZLE

6

JUMBLE®

Unscramble these four Jumbles, one letter to each square, to form four ordinary words.

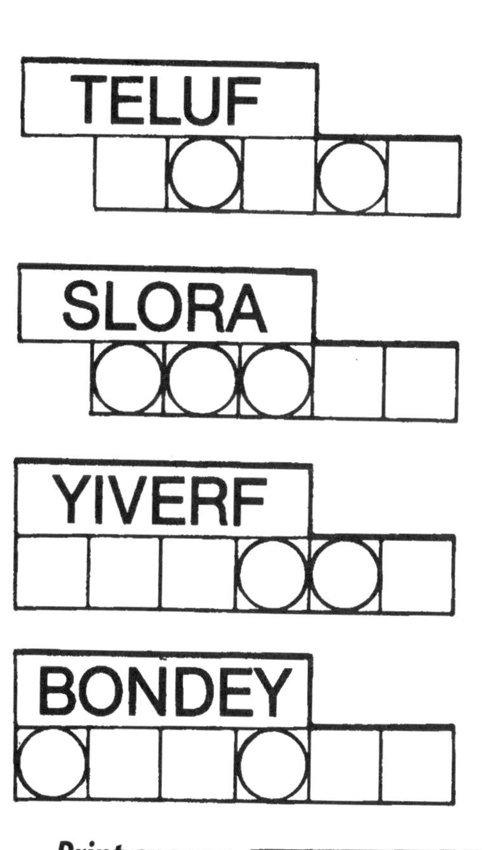

Now arrange the circled letters to form the surprise answer, as suggested by the above cartoon.

Print answer here ○○○○○ THE ○○○○

JUMBLE®

Unscramble these four Jumbles, one letter to each square, to form four ordinary words.

Now arrange the circled letters to form the surprise answer, as suggested by the above cartoon.

Print answer here " , ?"

PUZZLE

8

JUMBLE®

Unscramble these four Jumbles, one letter to each square, to form four ordinary words.

MAORA
ERQUE
RABENN
RATTEP
Never know what she's going to serve
HOW MANY TIMES WAS THE "PET MENU" REVISED?

Now arrange the circled letters to form the surprise answer, as suggested by the above cartoon.

Print answer here " "

PUZZLE

9

JUMBLE®

Unscramble these four Jumbles, one letter to each square, to form four ordinary words.

Now arrange the circled letters to form the surprise answer, as suggested by the above cartoon.

Print answer here THE “ ”

PUZZLE

10

JUMBLE®

Unscramble these four Jumbles, one letter to each square, to form four ordinary words.

Now arrange the circled letters to form the surprise answer, as suggested by the above cartoon.

Print answer here A

PUZZLE

11

JUMBLE®

Unscramble these four Jumbles, one letter to each square, to form four ordinary words.

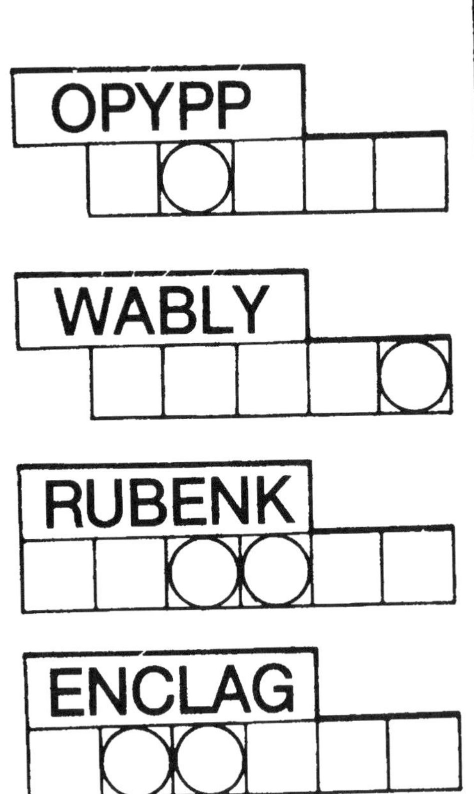

Now arrange the circled letters to form the surprise answer, as suggested by the above cartoon.

Print answer here 

PUZZLE

12

JUMBLE®

Unscramble these four Jumbles, one letter to each square, to form four ordinary words.

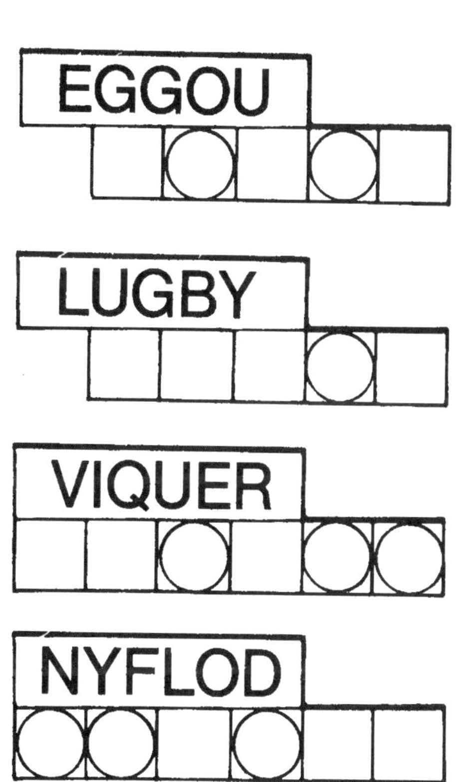
EGGOU
LUGBY
VIQUER
NYFLOD

He seems to be ENJOYING his suffering
WHAT THE HYPOCHONDRIAC'S MOTTO WAS.

Now arrange the circled letters to form the surprise answer, as suggested by the above cartoon.

Print answer here

PUZZLE

13

JUMBLE®

Unscramble these four Jumbles, one letter to each square, to form four ordinary words.

Now arrange the circled letters to form the surprise answer, as suggested by the above cartoon.

Print answer here

JUMBLE®

Unscramble these four Jumbles, one letter to each square, to form four ordinary words.

Now arrange the circled letters to form the surprise answer, as suggested by the above cartoon.

Print answer here A " "

PUZZLE

15

JUMBLE®

Unscramble these four Jumbles, one letter to each square, to form four ordinary words.

Now arrange the circled letters to form the surprise answer, as suggested by the above cartoon.

Print answer here " _ _ _ _ _ _ _ _ _ !"

PUZZLE

16

JUMBLE®
Unscramble these four Jumbles, one letter to each square, to form four ordinary words.
USIGE
INJOG
LEMDEY
NULKIE
THERE WAS PLENTY OF THIS WHEN A QUARREL BROKE OUT IN THE PIGPEN.
Now arrange the circled letters to form the surprise answer, as suggested by the above cartoon.
Print answer here

PUZZLE

17

JUMBLE®

Unscramble these four Jumbles, one letter to each square, to form four ordinary words.

Now arrange the circled letters to form the surprise answer, as suggested by the above cartoon.

Print answer here " ◯◯◯◯◯◯◯◯ "

PUZZLE

18

JUMBLE®

Unscramble these four Jumbles, one letter to each square, to form four ordinary words.

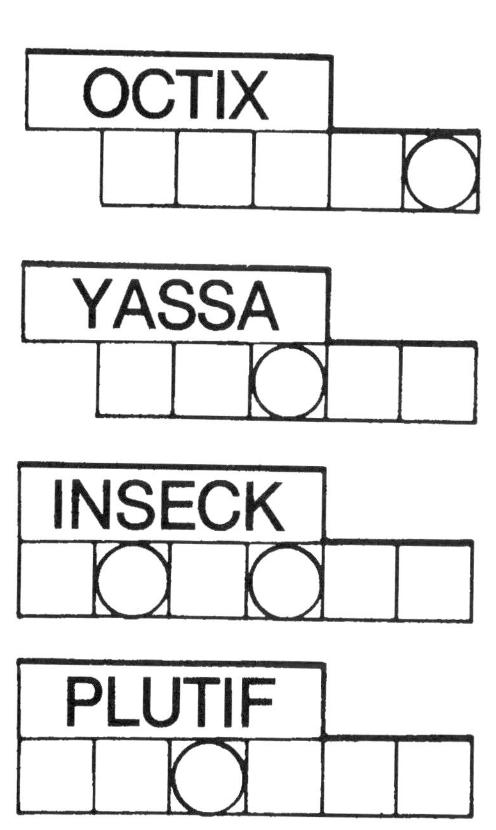

Now arrange the circled letters to form the surprise answer, as suggested by the above cartoon.

Print answer here "  "

PUZZLE

19

JUMBLE®

Unscramble these four Jumbles, one letter to each square, to form four ordinary words.

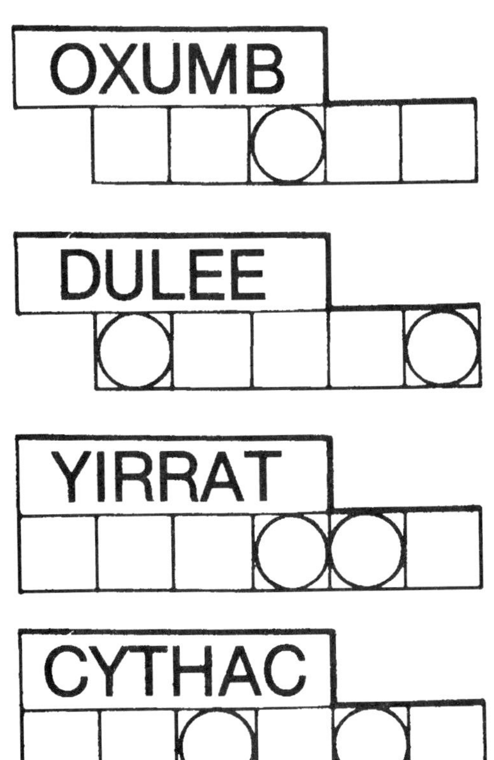

Now arrange the circled letters to form the surprise answer, as suggested by the above cartoon.

Print answer here 

JUMBLE®

Unscramble these four Jumbles, one letter to each square, to form four ordinary words.

KOYSM
VABOE
FRAITY
REFLAT
Get someone in to cook in the morning
IF YOU BREAK AN ARM, SOMEONE MIGHT HAVE TO MAKE THIS FOR YOU.

Now arrange the circled letters to form the surprise answer, as suggested by the above cartoon.

Print answer here THE " "

PUZZLE

21

JUMBLE®

Unscramble these four Jumbles, one letter to each square, to form four ordinary words.

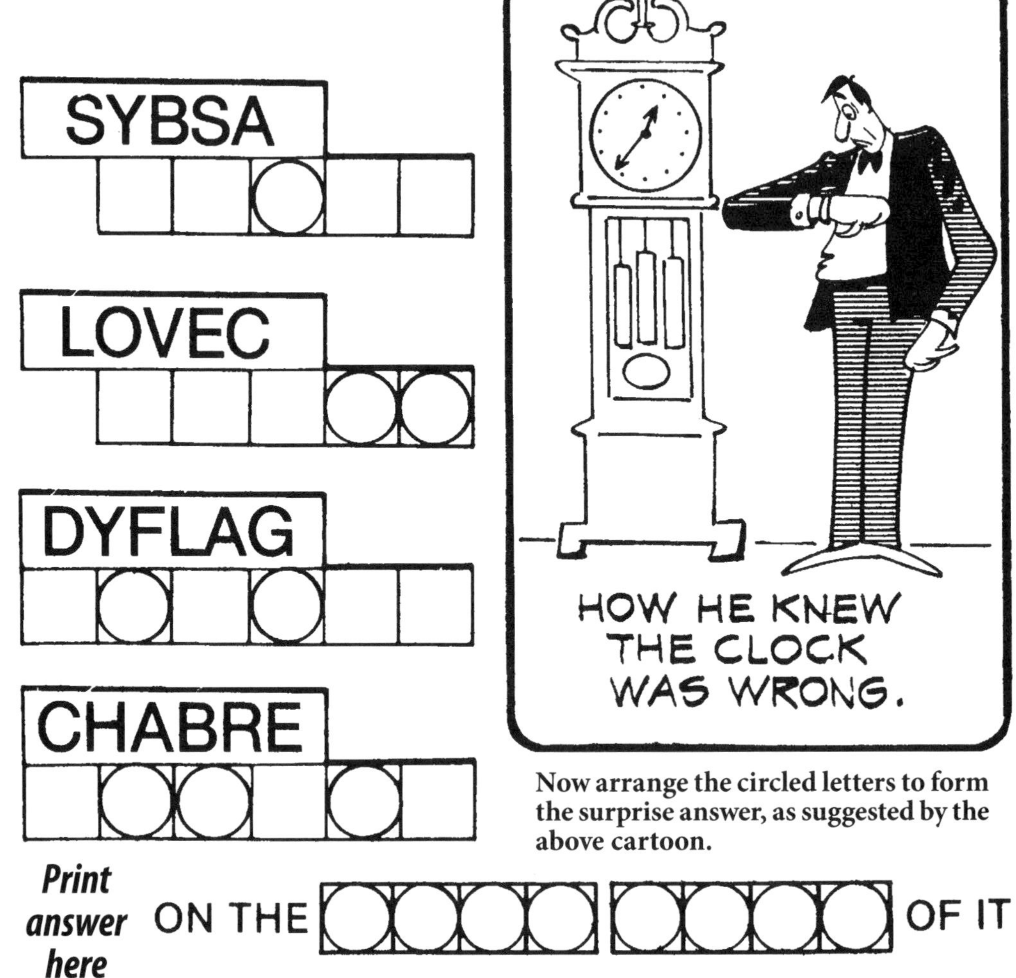

Now arrange the circled letters to form the surprise answer, as suggested by the above cartoon.

Print answer here ON THE ◯◯◯◯ ◯◯◯◯ OF IT

JUMBLE®

Unscramble these four Jumbles, one letter to each square, to form four ordinary words.

Now arrange the circled letters to form the surprise answer, as suggested by the above cartoon.

Print answer here " "

JUMBLE®

Unscramble these four Jumbles, one letter to each square, to form four ordinary words.

Now arrange the circled letters to form the surprise answer, as suggested by the above cartoon.

Print answer here

JUMBLE®

Unscramble these four Jumbles, one letter to each square, to form four ordinary words.

Now arrange the circled letters to form the surprise answer, as suggested by the above cartoon.

Print answer here

JUMBLE®

Unscramble these four Jumbles, one letter to each square, to form four ordinary words.

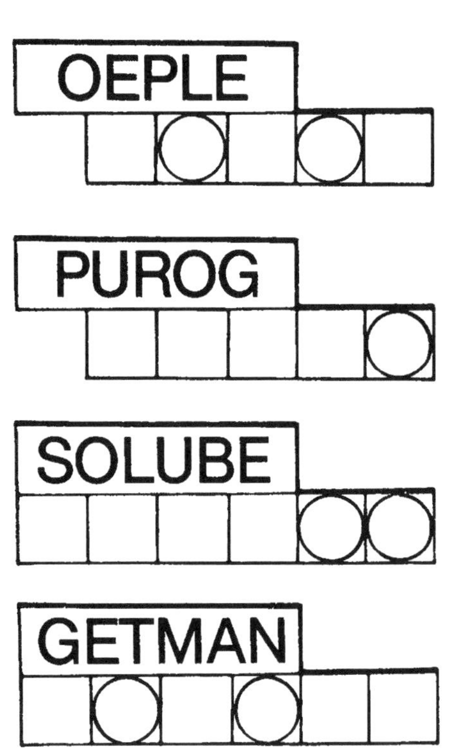

Now arrange the circled letters to form the surprise answer, as suggested by the above cartoon.

Print answer here

JUMBLE®

Cuisine

Daily Puzzles

JUMBLE®

Unscramble these four Jumbles, one letter to each square, to form four ordinary words.

Now arrange the circled letters to form the surprise answer, as suggested by the above cartoon.

Print answer here "◯◯◯◯ ME A ◯◯◯◯"

JUMBLE®

Unscramble these four Jumbles, one letter to each square, to form four ordinary words.

Now arrange the circled letters to form the surprise answer, as suggested by the above cartoon.

Print answer here ◯◯◯◯◯ A ◯◯◯◯

JUMBLE®

Unscramble these four Jumbles, one letter to each square, to form four ordinary words.

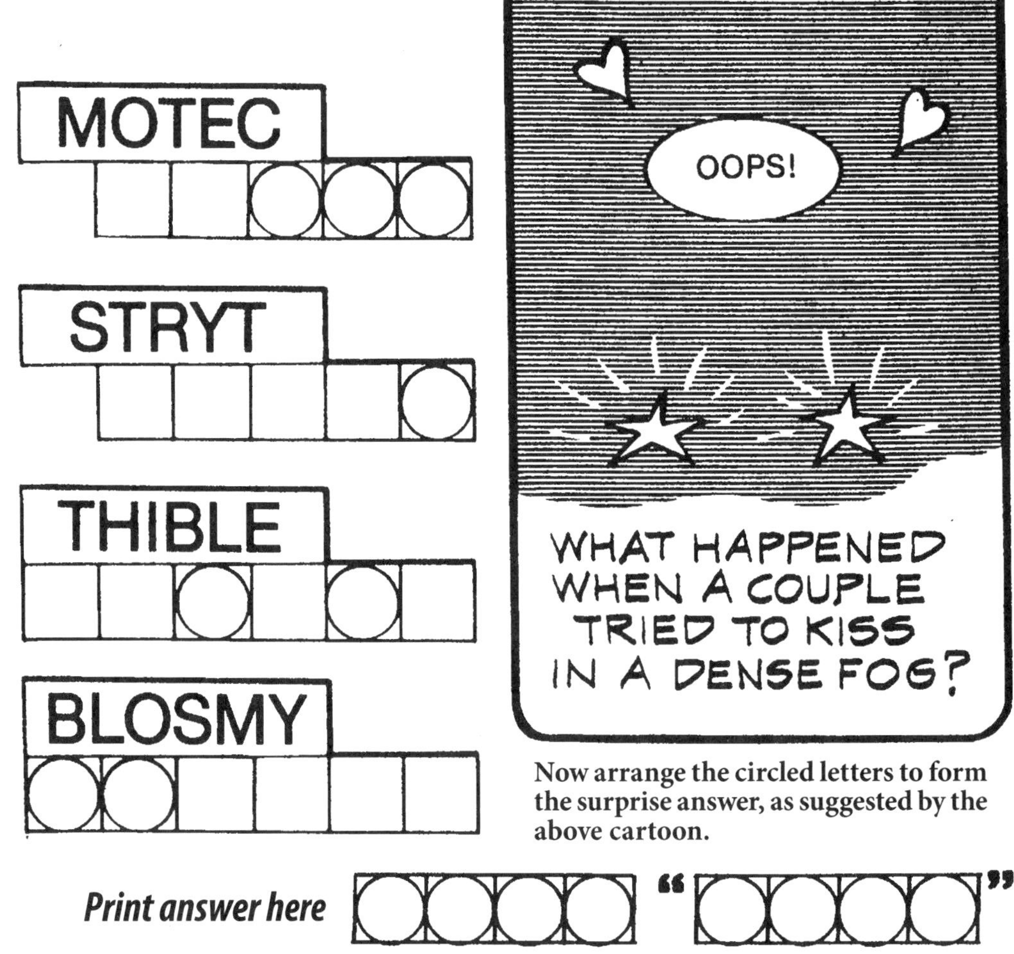

Now arrange the circled letters to form the surprise answer, as suggested by the above cartoon.

Print answer here "   "

PUZZLE

29

JUMBLE®

Unscramble these four Jumbles, one letter to each square, to form four ordinary words.

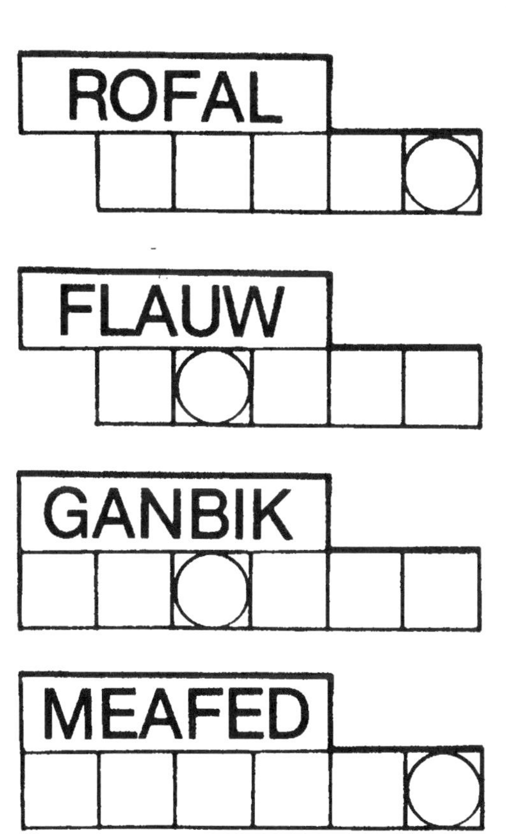

Now arrange the circled letters to form the surprise answer, as suggested by the above cartoon.

Print answer here 

JUMBLE®

Unscramble these four Jumbles, one letter to each square, to form four ordinary words.

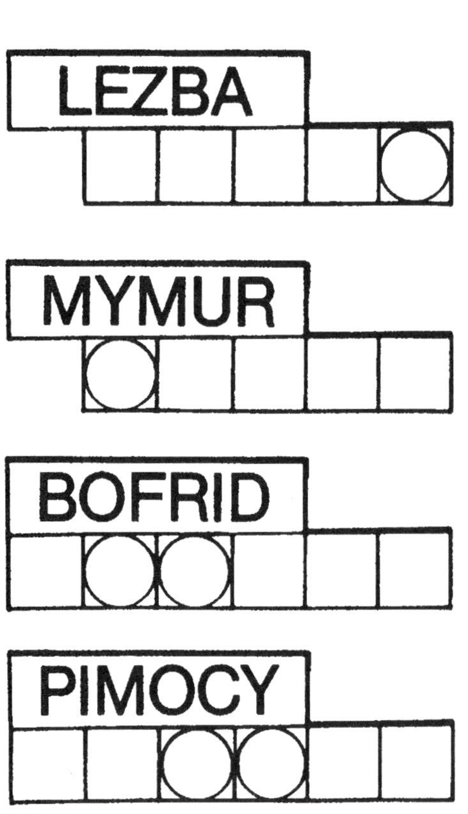
LEZBA
MYMUR
BOFRID
PIMOCY

I've had it!
WHAT POKER MAKES A POOR PLAYER.

Now arrange the circled letters to form the surprise answer, as suggested by the above cartoon.

Print answer here 

JUMBLE®

Unscramble these four Jumbles, one letter to each square, to form four ordinary words.

LUGIT
TAXEC
PEMEXT
WARROH
PRICES
LAMB . . . $9.80 lb.
BRISKET . . . $14.95 lb.
PORK . . . $8.95 lb.
VEAL . . $16.95 lb.
$
A BUTCHER IS A MAN LEAST LIKELY TO PUT ON THIS.

Now arrange the circled letters to form the surprise answer, as suggested by the above cartoon.

Print answer here

JUMBLE®

Unscramble these four Jumbles, one letter to each square, to form four ordinary words.

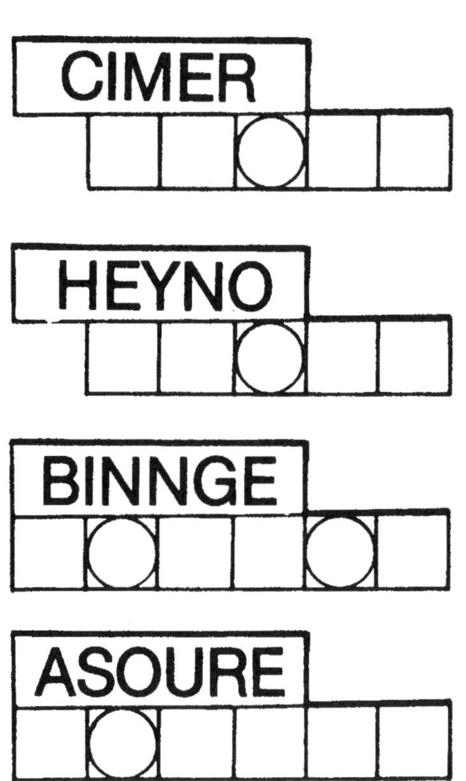

Now arrange the circled letters to form the surprise answer, as suggested by the above cartoon.

Print answer here A "◯◯◯◯◯"

PUZZLE

33

JUMBLE®

Unscramble these four Jumbles, one letter to each square, to form four ordinary words.

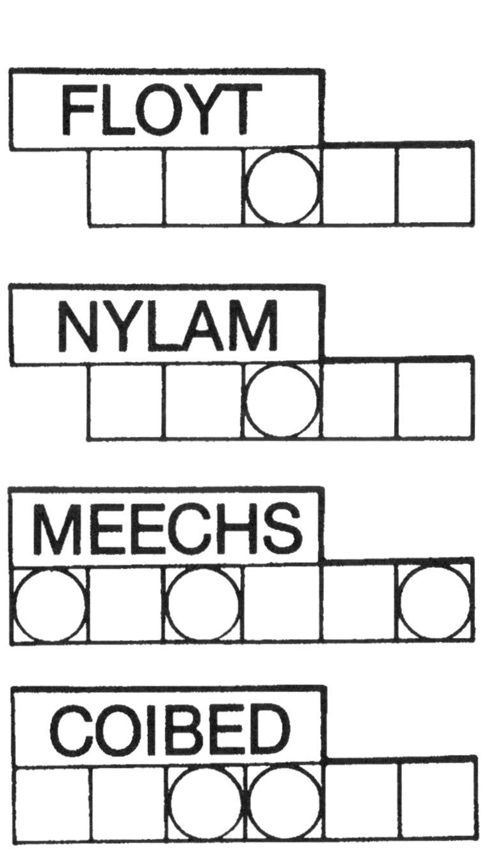

Now arrange the circled letters to form the surprise answer, as suggested by the above cartoon.

Print answer here AS  THEM

JUMBLE®

Unscramble these four Jumbles, one letter to each square, to form four ordinary words.

GUCOH
MUJOB
BELUCK
WHOANY
Ugh!
WHAT THAT INVISIBLE MAN DEFINITELY WAS NOT.

Now arrange the circled letters to form the surprise answer, as suggested by the above cartoon.

Print answer here ◯◯◯◯ TO ◯◯◯◯ AT

PUZZLE

35

JUMBLE®

Unscramble these four Jumbles, one letter to each square, to form four ordinary words.

CASIB
YAVEH
YAXTIL
BALIVE
He's already talked twice as long as he should have
THEY STRONGLY FELT THAT THE FILIBUSTERER SHOULD DO THIS.

Now arrange the circled letters to form the surprise answer, as suggested by the above cartoon.

Print answer here " ◯◯◯◯◯ " HIS ◯◯◯

PUZZLE

36

JUMBLE®

Unscramble these four Jumbles, one letter to each square, to form four ordinary words.

CREMY
REDON
PYSEDE
CASIMO
THAT GOSSIPY DRESS-MAKER APPEARED TO KNOW ONLY THIS ABOUT LIFE.

Now arrange the circled letters to form the surprise answer, as suggested by the above cartoon.

Print answer here THE " "

PUZZLE

37

JUMBLE®

Unscramble these four Jumbles, one letter to each square, to form four ordinary words.

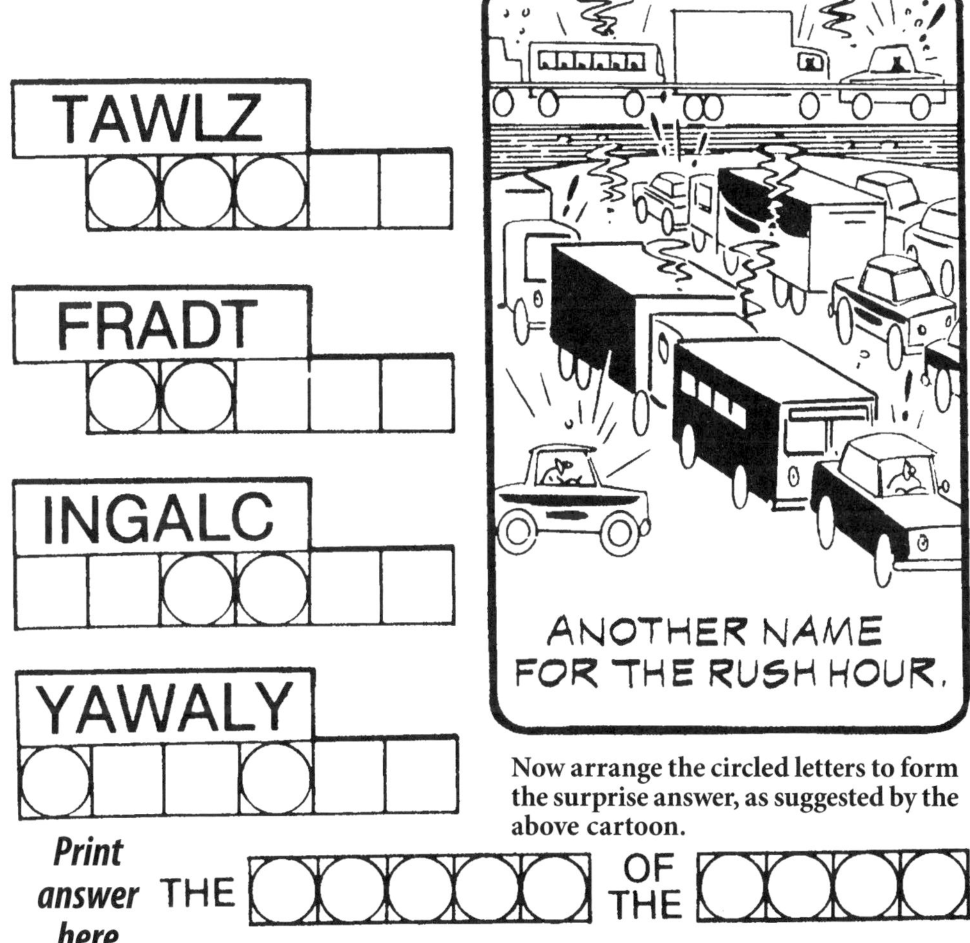
TAWLZ
FRADT
INGALC
YAWALY
ANOTHER NAME FOR THE RUSH HOUR.
Print answer here
THE
OF THE

Now arrange the circled letters to form the surprise answer, as suggested by the above cartoon.

JUMBLE®

Unscramble these four Jumbles, one letter to each square, to form four ordinary words.

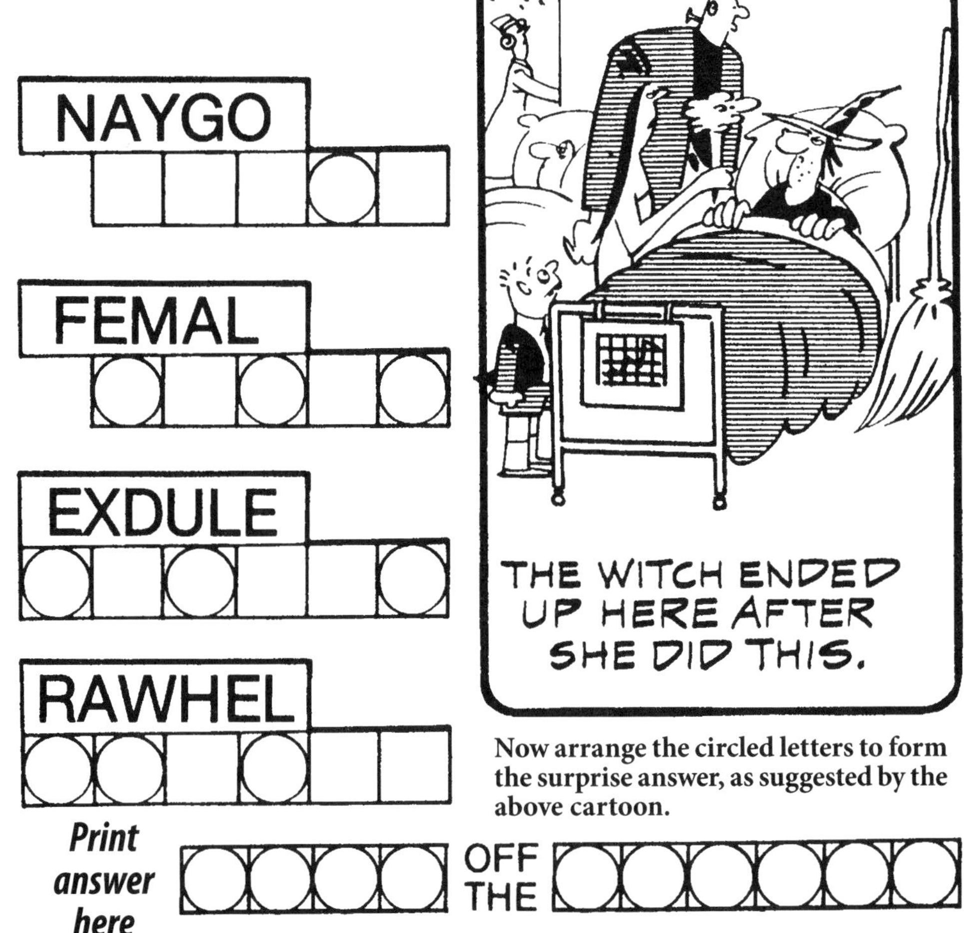
NAYGO
FEMAL
EXDULE
RAWHEL
THE WITCH ENDED UP HERE AFTER SHE DID THIS.
Now arrange the circled letters to form the surprise answer, as suggested by the above cartoon.
Print answer here
OFF THE

JUMBLE®

Unscramble these four Jumbles, one letter to each square, to form four ordinary words.

Now arrange the circled letters to form the surprise answer, as suggested by the above cartoon.

Print answer here " "

JUMBLE®

Unscramble these four Jumbles, one letter to each square, to form four ordinary words.

Now arrange the circled letters to form the surprise answer, as suggested by the above cartoon.

Print answer here " ◯◯◯ - ◯◯◯◯◯◯ "

PUZZLE

41

JUMBLE®
Unscramble these four Jumbles, one letter to each square, to form four ordinary words.
YUINT
NOLFE
KLUSCE
SLIFSO
WHAT SOME SKIERS JUMP TO.
Now arrange the circled letters to form the surprise answer, as suggested by the above cartoon.
Print answer here “ ”

JUMBLE®

Unscramble these four Jumbles, one letter to each square, to form four ordinary words.

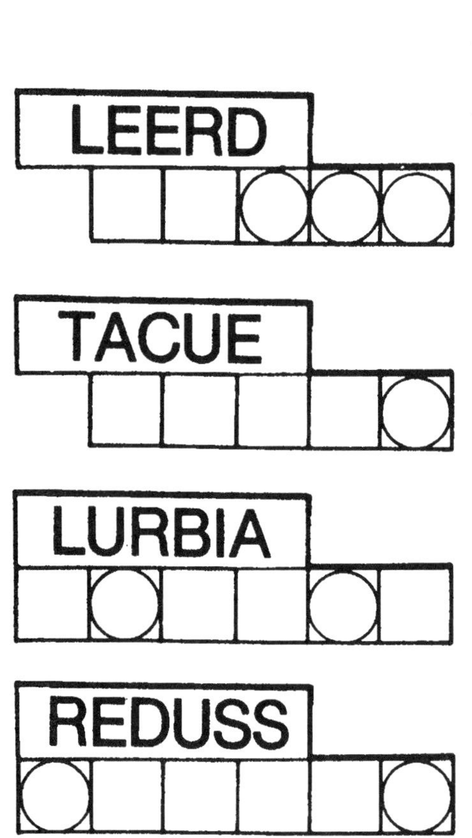
LEERD
TACUE
LURBIA
REDUSS

IT'S BETTER TO BE DEAD SURE AT A RAILROAD CROSSING THAN THIS.

Now arrange the circled letters to form the surprise answer, as suggested by the above cartoon.

Print answer here 

PUZZLE

43

JUMBLE®

Unscramble these four Jumbles, one letter to each square, to form four ordinary words.

Now arrange the circled letters to form the surprise answer, as suggested by the above cartoon.

Print answer here MORE ◯◯◯◯ THAN ◯◯◯' ◯◯

JUMBLE®

Unscramble these four Jumbles, one letter to each square, to form four ordinary words.

Now arrange the circled letters to form the surprise answer, as suggested by the above cartoon.

Print answer here ○○○○ OVER ○○○○

PUZZLE

45

JUMBLE®

Unscramble these four Jumbles, one letter to each square, to form four ordinary words.

CYKAT
RUGPO
FASTIE
ENOMAY
DISCO
He owns the place, too
WHAT YOU MIGHT SEE A BOUNCER THROW.

Now arrange the circled letters to form the surprise answer, as suggested by the above cartoon.

Print answer here A

PUZZLE

46

JUMBLE®

Unscramble these four Jumbles, one letter to each square, to form four ordinary words.

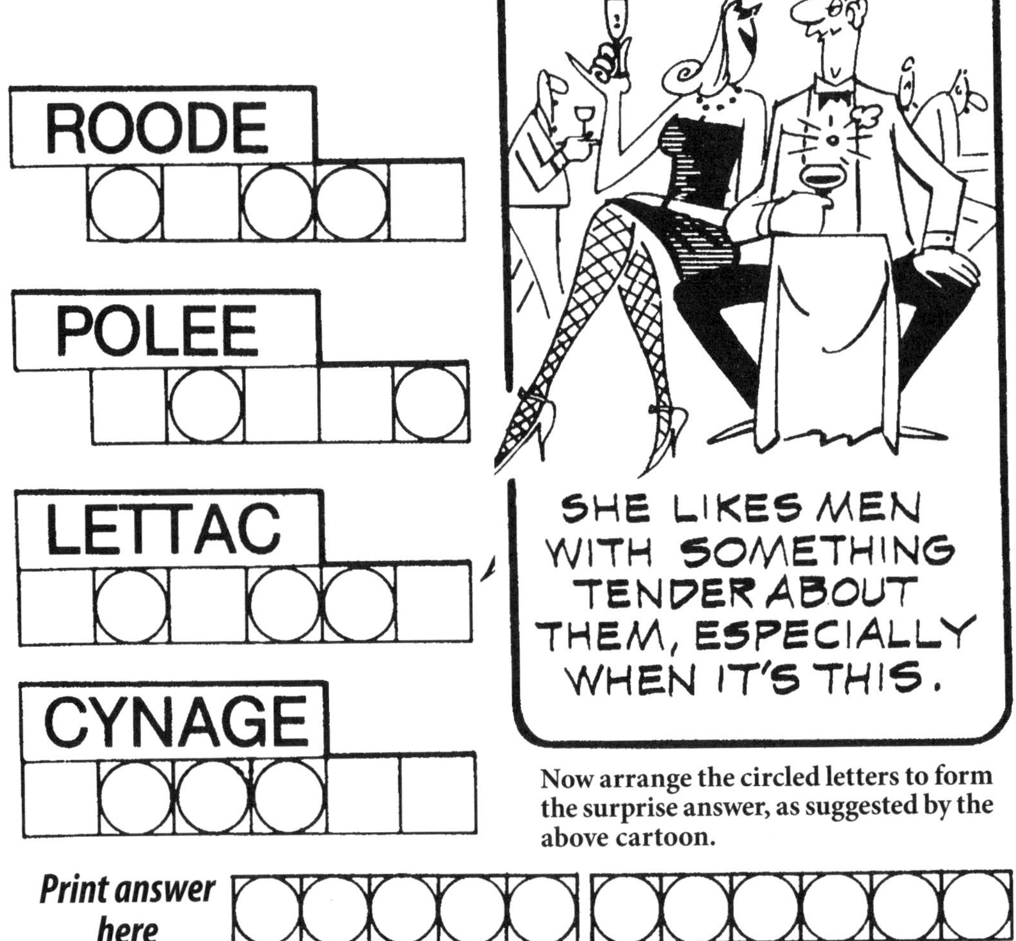

Now arrange the circled letters to form the surprise answer, as suggested by the above cartoon.

Print answer here

PUZZLE

47

JUMBLE®

Unscramble these four Jumbles, one letter to each square, to form four ordinary words.

Now arrange the circled letters to form the surprise answer, as suggested by the above cartoon.

Print answer here

“ - ”

PUZZLE

48

JUMBLE®

Unscramble these four Jumbles, one letter to each square, to form four ordinary words.

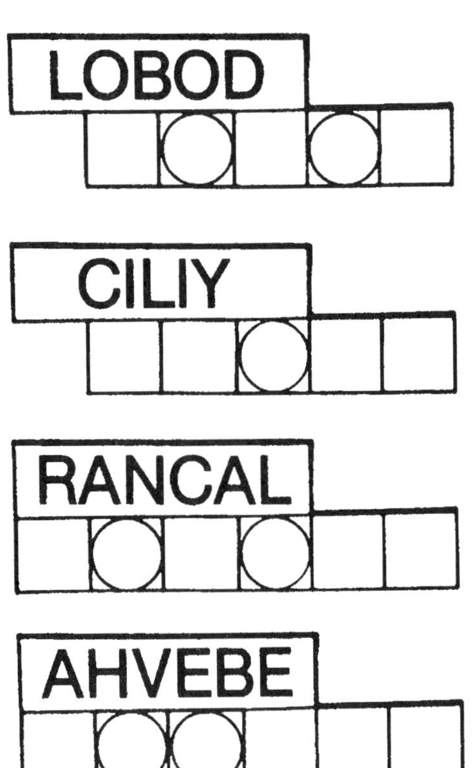

Now arrange the circled letters to form the surprise answer, as suggested by the above cartoon.

Print answer here 

JUMBLE®

Unscramble these four Jumbles, one letter to each square, to form four ordinary words.

RONOC
BIRAB
ENTABE
JEDAGG
Last year she said she was twenty-nine
AT THIRTY A WOMAN IS OFTEN AS OLD AS THIS.

Now arrange the circled letters to form the surprise answer, as suggested by the above cartoon.

Print answer here SHE'S

JUMBLE®

Unscramble these four Jumbles, one letter to each square, to form four ordinary words.

VIRTE
RETEB
BORREB
HYLLOW
It's supposed to be a wall
HOW A MASON LEARNS HIS TRADE.

Now arrange the circled letters to form the surprise answer, as suggested by the above cartoon.

Print answer here BY " " &

PUZZLE 51

JUMBLE®

Unscramble these four Jumbles, one letter to each square, to form four ordinary words.

STOIF
HOACS
MAGITS
YULOHN
Come and get me!
WHAT THE GUY WHO BRUSHED HIS TEETH WITH GUNPOWDER DID.
Now arrange the circled letters to form the surprise answer, as suggested by the above cartoon.
Print answer here
HIS
OFF

PUZZLE

52

JUMBLE®

Unscramble these four Jumbles, one letter to each square, to form four ordinary words.

Now arrange the circled letters to form the surprise answer, as suggested by the above cartoon.

Print answer here " "

JUMBLE®

Unscramble these four Jumbles, one letter to each square, to form four ordinary words.

CHULG
PEALL
NULRUY
ENBAUT
WHAT THE GUY WHO WAS TRYING TO BE THE LIFE OF THE PARTY ACTUALLY MANAGED TO BE.
Now arrange the circled letters to form the surprise answer, as suggested by the above cartoon.
Print answer here
THE
OF THE

PUZZLE

54

JUMBLE®

Unscramble these four Jumbles, one letter to each square, to form four ordinary words.

PUTER
DUBON
LALCOW
FIFRAM
Go ahead—he won't bite you
PRIVATE
AN ENTERPRISING PERSON SHOULD NOT BE BACKWARD IN GOING THERE.
Print answer here

Now arrange the circled letters to form the surprise answer, as suggested by the above cartoon.

PUZZLE

55

JUMBLE®

Unscramble these four Jumbles, one letter to each square, to form four ordinary words.

RASEE

DICHE

RAHNGE

DIBITT

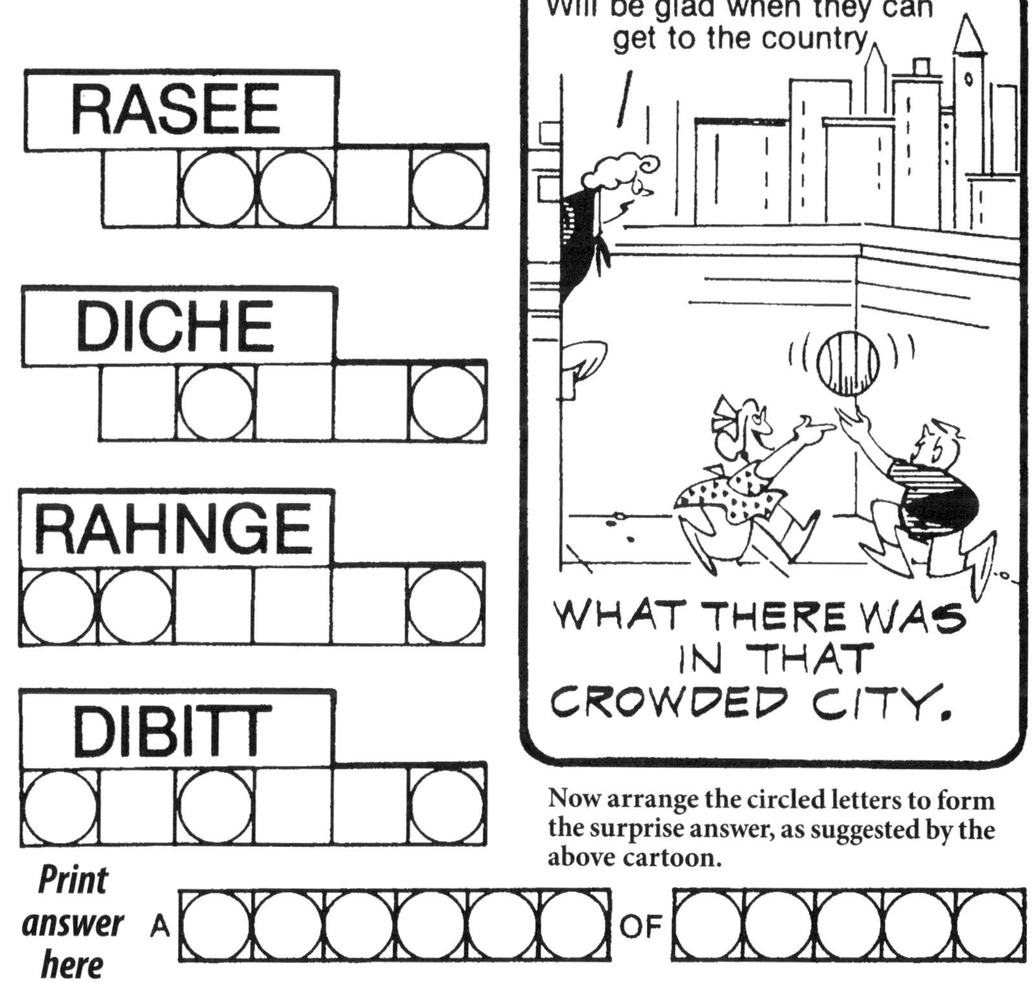

Now arrange the circled letters to form the surprise answer, as suggested by the above cartoon.

Print answer here A ○○○○○○ OF ○○○○○

PUZZLE

56

JUMBLE®

Unscramble these four Jumbles, one letter to each square, to form four ordinary words.

Now arrange the circled letters to form the surprise answer, as suggested by the above cartoon.

Print answer here " "

PUZZLE

57

JUMBLE®

Unscramble these four Jumbles, one letter to each square, to form four ordinary words.

RODUG

VORLE

ABBOMO

DURECE

Now arrange the circled letters to form the surprise answer, as suggested by the above cartoon.

Print answer here ONE ◯◯◯◯ TO "◯◯◯◯◯"

JUMBLE®

Unscramble these four Jumbles, one letter to each square, to form four ordinary words.

LUFTO
DENIK
UNCANE
BRUBRE
Yeah, I got all de angles
But just look at that guy!
EITHER A BOXER CARRIES OUT HIS PLANS TO BEAT HIS OPPONENT, OR HE'S THIS.

Now arrange the circled letters to form the surprise answer, as suggested by the above cartoon.

Print answer here

PUZZLE

59

JUMBLE®

Unscramble these four Jumbles, one letter to each square, to form four ordinary words.

YAARR
UFYSS
TRULSY
NARROC
THE BEST WAY TO MAKE UP.
Now arrange the circled letters to form the surprise answer, as suggested by the above cartoon.
Print answer here
YOU'RE

PUZZLE

60

JUMBLE®

Unscramble these four Jumbles, one letter to each square, to form four ordinary words.

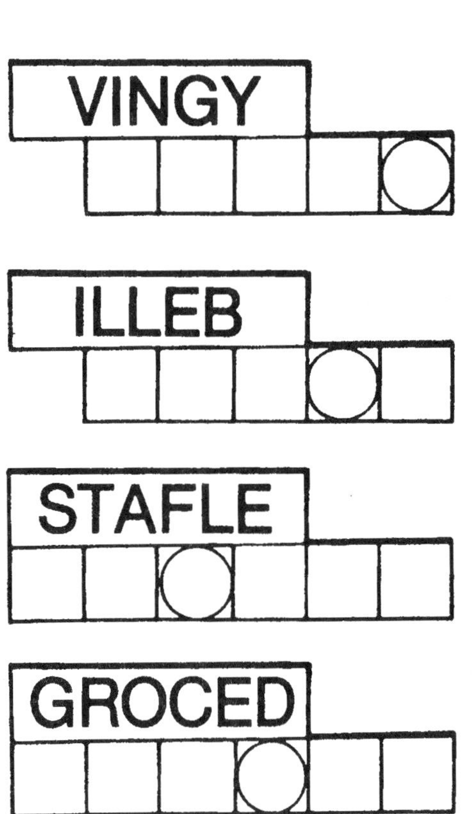

Now arrange the circled letters to form the surprise answer, as suggested by the above cartoon.

Print answer here 

PUZZLE

61

JUMBLE®
Unscramble these four Jumbles, one letter to each square, to form four ordinary words.
DIPTE
KLUSK
TOOWWK
RANLYX
He sure knows all the angles
WHAT THE GEOGRAPHER WAS, NATURALLY.

Now arrange the circled letters to form the surprise answer, as suggested by the above cartoon.

Print answer here " ◯◯◯◯◯◯◯ " ◯◯◯◯

PUZZLE

62

JUMBLE®

Unscramble these four Jumbles, one letter to each square, to form four ordinary words.

Now arrange the circled letters to form the surprise answer, as suggested by the above cartoon.

Print answer here

PUZZLE

63

JUMBLE®

Unscramble these four Jumbles, one letter to each square, to form four ordinary words.

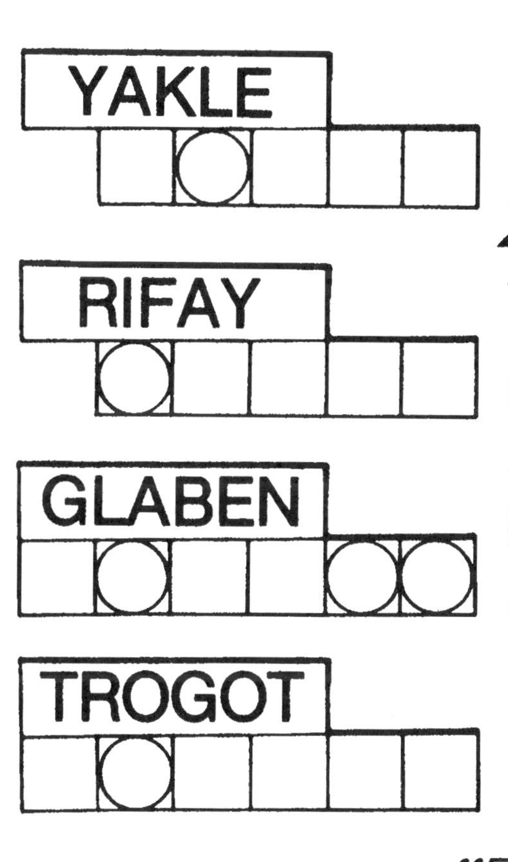

YAKLE
RIFAY
GLABEN
TROGOT

So glad that cold spell is over
WHAT SPRING SHOULD BRING AFTER A ROUGH WINTER.

Now arrange the circled letters to form the surprise answer, as suggested by the above cartoon.

Print answer here " - "

JUMBLE®

Unscramble these four Jumbles, one letter to each square, to form four ordinary words.

PUZZLE

65

JUMBLE®

Unscramble these four Jumbles, one letter to each square, to form four ordinary words.

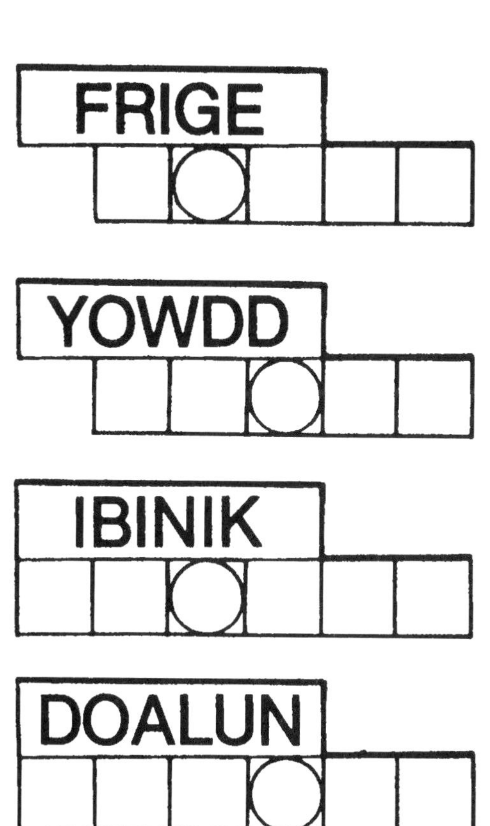

Now arrange the circled letters to form the surprise answer, as suggested by the above cartoon.

Print answer here 

JUMBLE®

Unscramble these four Jumbles, one letter to each square, to form four ordinary words.

PUZZLE

67

JUMBLE®
Unscramble these four Jumbles, one letter to each square, to form four ordinary words.
BRUTS
NOKTE
NAANAB
YENITT
Name your weapon!
WHAT HE SAID WHEN HE WAS CHALLENGED TO A DUEL.

Now arrange the circled letters to form the surprise answer, as suggested by the above cartoon.

Print answer here "I'LL [ ][ ][ ][ ] A [ ][ ][ ][ ] AT IT"

PUZZLE

68

JUMBLE®

Unscramble these four Jumbles, one letter to each square, to form four ordinary words.

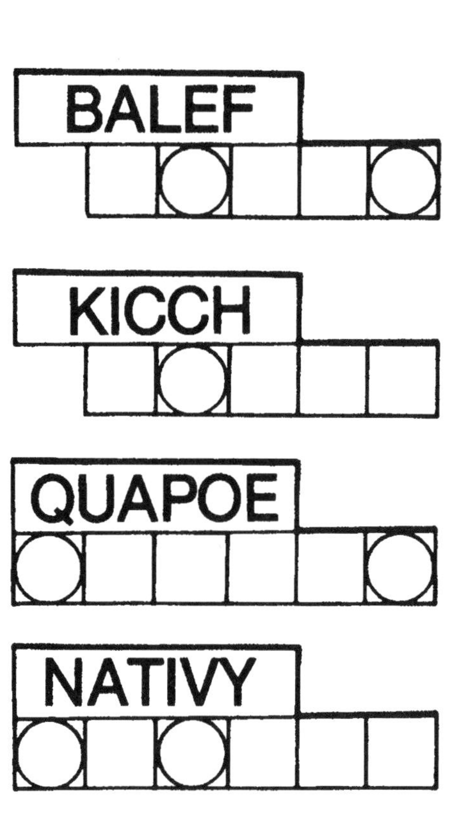
BALEF
KICCH
QUAPOE
NATIVY

He may be overdoing it
APPARENTLY, A GUY WHO EATS AND DRINKS TOO MUCH WOULD RATHER BE A GOOD LIVER THAN THIS.

Now arrange the circled letters to form the surprise answer, as suggested by the above cartoon.

Print answer here 

PUZZLE

69

JUMBLE®

Unscramble these four Jumbles, one letter to each square, to form four ordinary words.

Now arrange the circled letters to form the surprise answer, as suggested by the above cartoon.

Print answer here A ◯◯◯◯◯ "◯◯◯◯"

JUMBLE®

Unscramble these four Jumbles, one letter to each square, to form four ordinary words.

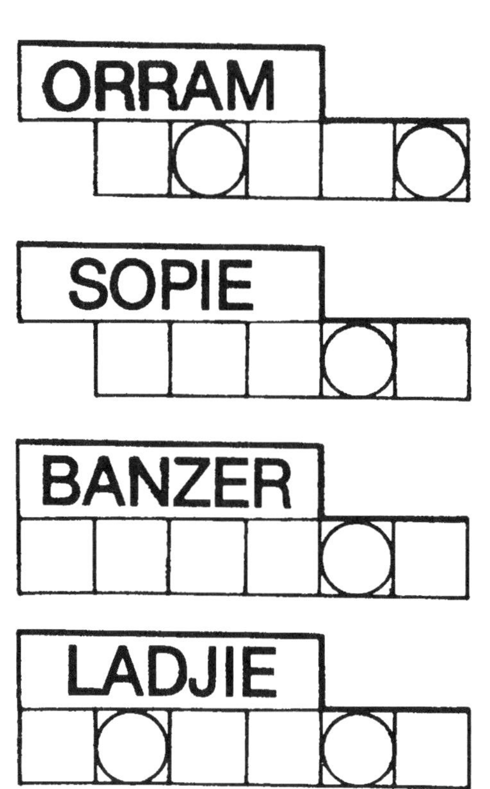
ORRAM
SOPIE
BANZER
LADJIE

PRO SHOP
THIS HELPS MANY A GOLFER TO IMPROVE HIS SCORE.

Now arrange the circled letters to form the surprise answer, as suggested by the above cartoon.

Print answer here AN 

PUZZLE

71

JUMBLE®

Unscramble these four Jumbles, one letter to each square, to form four ordinary words.

ZOTAP
CUFOS
CULTOC
SPYNAP
TOP SECRET
WHAT KIND OF GLASSES DO FOREIGN AGENTS WEAR?

Now arrange the circled letters to form the surprise answer, as suggested by the above cartoon.

Print answer here " ○○○ - ○○○○○○ "

PUZZLE

72

JUMBLE®

Unscramble these four Jumbles, one letter to each square, to form four ordinary words.

PUZZLE

73

JUMBLE®

Unscramble these four Jumbles, one letter to each square, to form four ordinary words.

CUTHE
DILAY
SEECIX
YASUNE
WHAT THE PHOTOGENIC MOUSE KNEW HOW TO DO VERY WELL.

Now arrange the circled letters to form the surprise answer, as suggested by the above cartoon.

Print answer here

PUZZLE

74

JUMBLE®

Unscramble these four Jumbles, one letter to each square, to form four ordinary words.

BALOT
TULXE
BANDOU
ROSIAL
They'll never wear out
WHAT A GOOD PAIR OF HANDMADE SHOES SHOULD BE.
Now arrange the circled letters to form the surprise answer, as suggested by the above cartoon.
Print answer here
TO " "

JUMBLE®

Unscramble these four Jumbles, one letter to each square, to form four ordinary words.

Now arrange the circled letters to form the surprise answer, as suggested by the above cartoon.

Print answer here OUT OF

PUZZLE

76

JUMBLE®

Unscramble these four Jumbles, one letter to each square, to form four ordinary words.

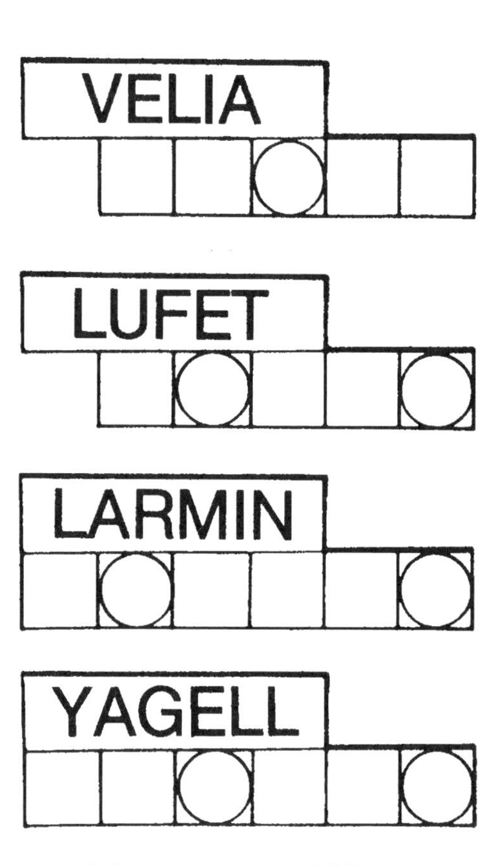

Now arrange the circled letters to form the surprise answer, as suggested by the above cartoon.

Print answer here  IT ON THE 

JUMBLE®

Unscramble these four Jumbles, one letter to each square, to form four ordinary words.

MYOFA
JEGUD
HEWZEE
TORMAN
Wait'll they see the results of these exams!
WHERE THE GEOLOGY PRO-FESSOR BROUGHT HIS STUDENTS.

Now arrange the circled letters to form the surprise answer, as suggested by the above cartoon.

Print answer here ◯◯◯◯ TO ◯◯◯◯◯

JUMBLE®

Unscramble these four Jumbles, one letter to each square, to form four ordinary words.

NOCOL

BOLEN

QULLAS

DIRTOR

Now arrange the circled letters to form the surprise answer, as suggested by the above cartoon.

Print answer here HER

PUZZLE

79

JUMBLE®

Unscramble these four Jumbles, one letter to each square, to form four ordinary words.

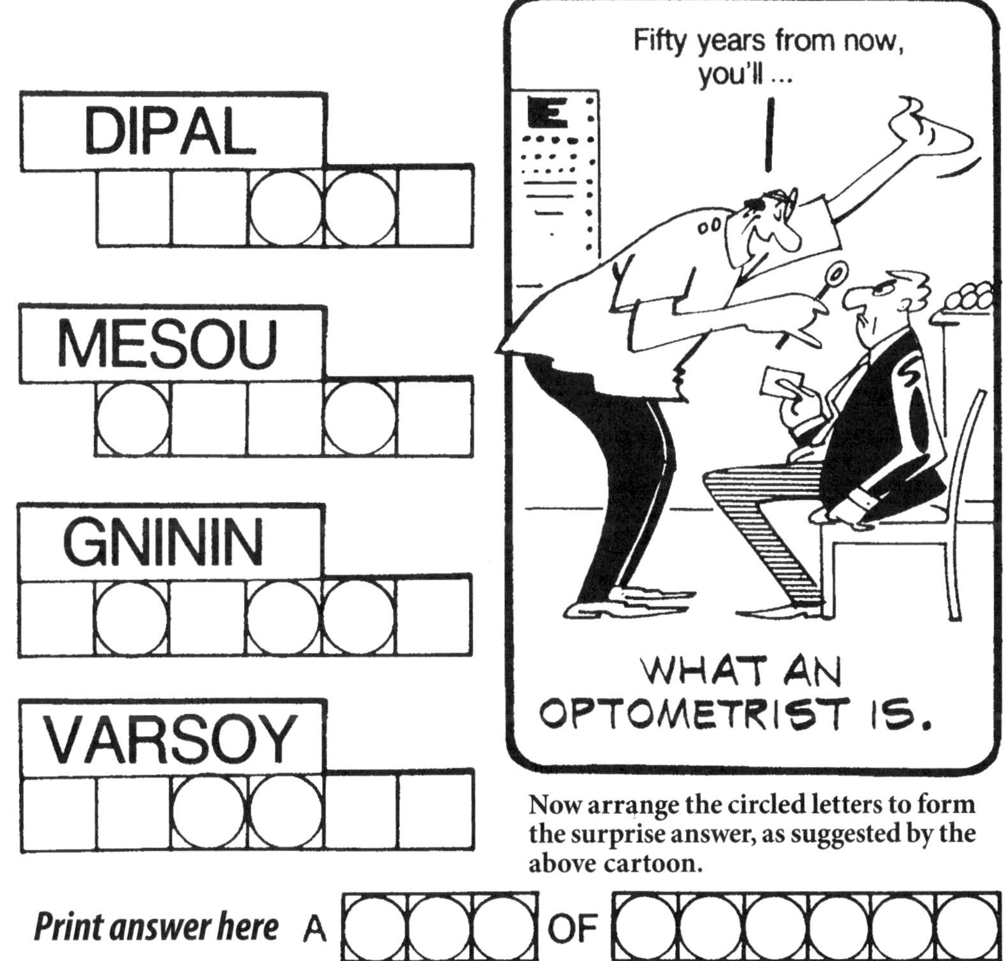

DIPAL
MESOU
GNININ
VARSOY
Fifty years from now, you'll ...
WHAT AN OPTOMETRIST IS.
Now arrange the circled letters to form the surprise answer, as suggested by the above cartoon.
Print answer here A OF

PUZZLE

80

JUMBLE®

Unscramble these four Jumbles, one letter to each square, to form four ordinary words.

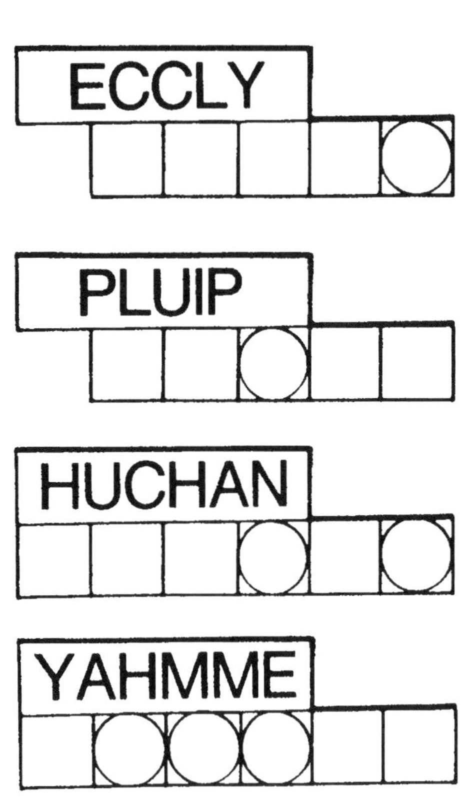

Now arrange the circled letters to form the surprise answer, as suggested by the above cartoon.

Print answer here

PUZZLE

81

JUMBLE®

Unscramble these four Jumbles, one letter to each square, to form four ordinary words.

Now arrange the circled letters to form the surprise answer, as suggested by the above cartoon.

Print answer here THE " ◯◯◯◯◯ " ◯◯◯◯◯◯

PUZZLE

82

JUMBLE®

Unscramble these four Jumbles, one letter to each square, to form four ordinary words.

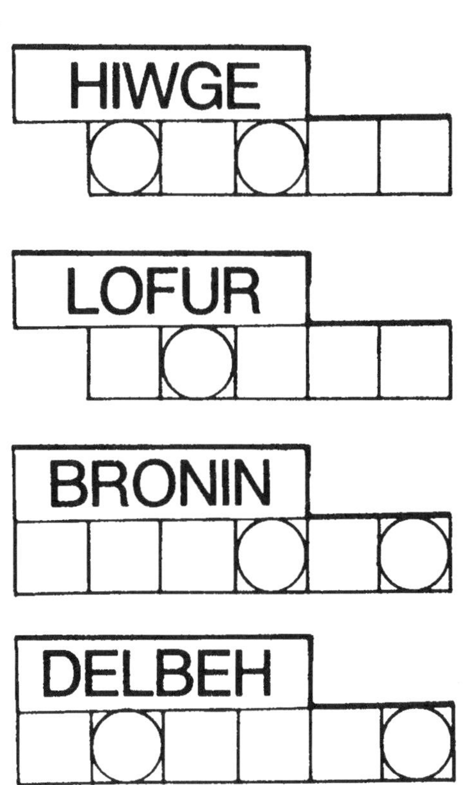

HIWGE
LOFUR
BRONIN
DELBEH

HE PICKED A SOFT JOB BECAUSE HE EXPECTED TO DO THIS LATER.

Now arrange the circled letters to form the surprise answer, as suggested by the above cartoon.

Print answer here

ON IT

JUMBLE®

Unscramble these four Jumbles, one letter to each square, to form four ordinary words.

KYMOS
GEGAU
ANFLOG
YIPRAC
CLASS OF '86
I guess this is what we've been looking forward to
WHAT GRADUATION TIME WAS FOR THOSE YOUNG PEOPLE.

Now arrange the circled letters to form the surprise answer, as suggested by the above cartoon.

Print answer here THE "◯◯◯◯◯" OF ◯◯◯◯◯

JUMBLE®

Unscramble these four Jumbles, one letter to each square, to form four ordinary words.

UGLIE

SNAIB

FRODIL

TEXCIE

SPECIALS TODAY:
Fried snakes
Broiled eels
Baked octopus
FOOD SOME PEOPLE FIND EDIBLE MIGHT SEEM THIS TO OTHERS.

Now arrange the circled letters to form the surprise answer, as suggested by the above cartoon.

Print answer here

PUZZLE

85

JUMBLE
Unscramble these four Jumbles, one letter to each square, to form four ordinary words.
VEDEL
KELUF
RAMAAD
LAPLID
I remember it as though it were yesterday
WHAT A PHOTO-GRAPHIC MEMORY NEVER SEEMS TO RUN OUT OF.

Now arrange the circled letters to form the surprise answer, as suggested by the above cartoon.

Print answer here

PUZZLE

86

JUMBLE®

Unscramble these four Jumbles, one letter to each square, to form four ordinary words.

JUMBLE®

Unscramble these four Jumbles, one letter to each square, to form four ordinary words.

GYROL
GURAU
FLENNE
CHISPY
Not much upstairs
But she can sure dance
WHAT A DANCER'S REPUTATION OFTEN RESTS UPON.

Now arrange the circled letters to form the surprise answer, as suggested by the above cartoon.

Print answer here

PUZZLE

88

JUMBLE®

Unscramble these four Jumbles, one letter to each square, to form four ordinary words.

NEPOR

INNOO

HEHRST

FITANN

Now arrange the circled letters to form the surprise answer, as suggested by the above cartoon.

Print answer here UP IN " "

PUZZLE

89

JUMBLE®

Unscramble these four Jumbles, one letter to each square, to form four ordinary words.

REPPA
MAGEL
GINDAR
BOSULE
His work has made him rich
HOW A PASTRY CHEF DOESN'T LIVE.
Now arrange the circled letters to form the surprise answer, as suggested by the above cartoon.
Print answer here BY

JUMBLE®

Unscramble these four Jumbles, one letter to each square, to form four ordinary words.

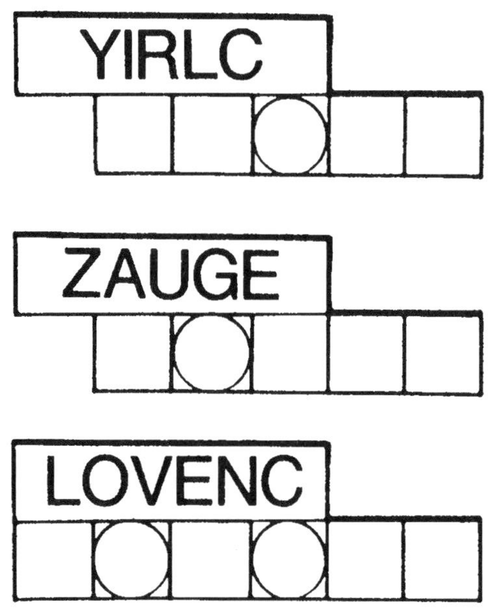
YIRLC
ZAUGE
LOVENC
GAFINC

You devil, you!
WHAT YOU WILL NEVER HAVE IF YOU FALL IN LOVE WITH YOURSELF.

Now arrange the circled letters to form the surprise answer, as suggested by the above cartoon.

Print answer here 

PUZZLE

91

JUMBLE®

Unscramble these four Jumbles, one letter to each square, to form four ordinary words.

Now arrange the circled letters to form the surprise answer, as suggested by the above cartoon.

Print answer here A "◯◯◯◯-◯◯" ONE

PUZZLE

92

JUMBLE®

Unscramble these four Jumbles, one letter to each square, to form four ordinary words.

Now arrange the circled letters to form the surprise answer, as suggested by the above cartoon.

Print answer here " "

PUZZLE

93

JUMBLE®

Unscramble these four Jumbles, one letter to each square, to form four ordinary words.

HIMEC
MESOO
BEEDAT
TRUXAS
I wouldn't trust him from here to the door
WHAT A POLITICIAN'S LIFE OFTEN IS.

Now arrange the circled letters to form the surprise answer, as suggested by the above cartoon.

Print answer here A ◯◯◯ OF “◯◯◯◯◯”

PUZZLE

94

JUMBLE®

Unscramble these four Jumbles, one letter to each square, to form four ordinary words.

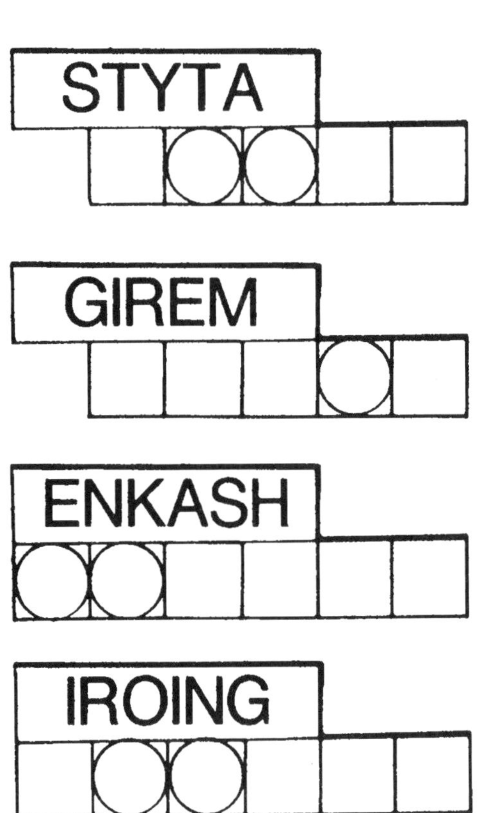

Now arrange the circled letters to form the surprise answer, as suggested by the above cartoon.

Print answer here WITH

PUZZLE

95

JUMBLE®

Unscramble these four Jumbles, one letter to each square, to form four ordinary words.

Now arrange the circled letters to form the surprise answer, as suggested by the above cartoon.

Print answer here

PUZZLE

96

JUMBLE®

Unscramble these four Jumbles, one letter to each square, to form four ordinary words.

Now arrange the circled letters to form the surprise answer, as suggested by the above cartoon.

Print answer here ☐☐☐☐☐ ON ☐☐☐☐

JUMBLE®

Unscramble these four Jumbles, one letter to each square, to form four ordinary words.

Now arrange the circled letters to form the surprise answer, as suggested by the above cartoon.

Print answer here

PUZZLE

98

JUMBLE®

Unscramble these four Jumbles, one letter to each square, to form four ordinary words.

REXET

DUGEF

STYMIC

NESTOL

Now arrange the circled letters to form the surprise answer, as suggested by the above cartoon.

Print answer here ◯◯◯◯ - ◯ "◯◯◯◯◯"

PUZZLE

99

JUMBLE®

Unscramble these four Jumbles, one letter to each square, to form four ordinary words.

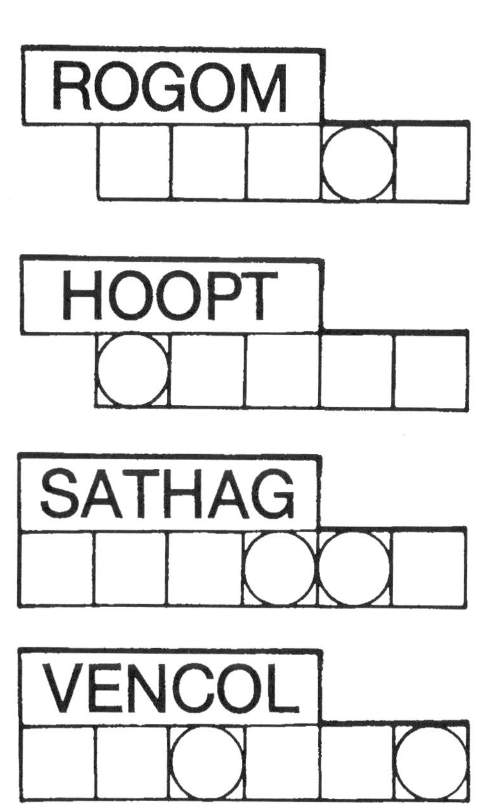

Now arrange the circled letters to form the surprise answer, as suggested by the above cartoon.

Print answer here "  "

PUZZLE

100

JUMBLE®

Unscramble these four Jumbles, one letter to each square, to form four ordinary words.

Now arrange the circled letters to form the surprise answer, as suggested by the above cartoon.

Print answer here THE

JUMBLE®

Unscramble these four Jumbles, one letter to each square, to form four ordinary words.

WPEST
SIYNO
TTIYRH
NPEAPH
I can't believe you fixed the storm damage so quickly. It looks great.
It's even better than before.
AFTER REPAIRS WERE MADE ON THE CHURCH SPIRE, IT WAS ---

Now arrange the circled letters to form the surprise answer, as suggested by the above cartoon.

Print answer here

JUMBLE®

Unscramble these four Jumbles, one letter to each square, to form four ordinary words.

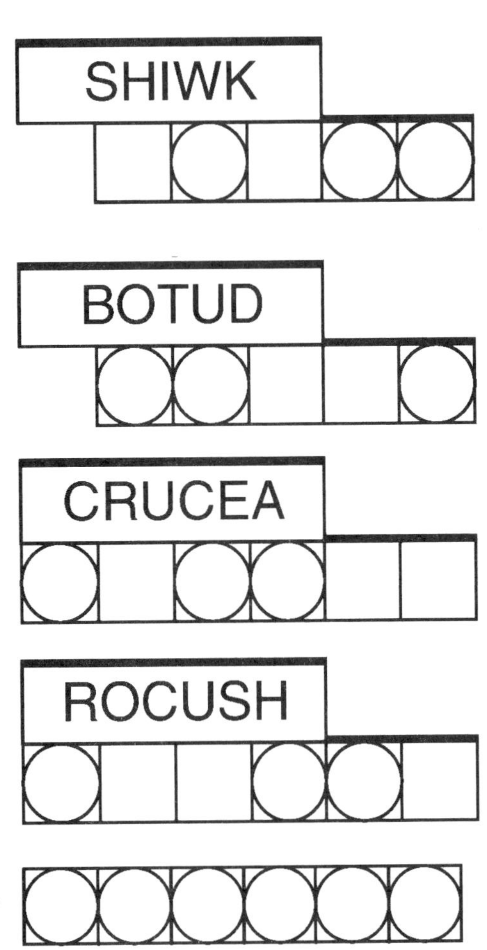

Now arrange the circled letters to form the surprise answer, as suggested by the above cartoon.

Print answer here

PUZZLE

103

JUMBLE®

Unscramble these four Jumbles, one letter to each square, to form four ordinary words.

ATVIL
OSITJ
CIPETD
GRUBER
This is the best cheese I've ever tasted!
You won't believe what I paid for it.
Yum!
AFTER USING A COUPON TO GET THE FANCY CHEESE AT 70 PERCENT OFF, THEY ---

Now arrange the circled letters to form the surprise answer, as suggested by the above cartoon.

Print answer here "◯◯◯◯◯-◯◯" ◯◯

JUMBLE®

Unscramble these four Jumbles, one letter to each square, to form four ordinary words.

Now arrange the circled letters to form the surprise answer, as suggested by the above cartoon.

Print answer here ◯◯◯'◯ ◯◯◯◯◯◯◯ ◯◯

JUMBLE®

Unscramble these four Jumbles, one letter to each square, to form four ordinary words.

VICLI
UCCHO
YELRAL
SETORE
I'm glad we're all giving to the relief efforts.
Everyone's so generous.
THE CHURCHGOERS PASSED AROUND THE OFFERING PLATE ---

Now arrange the circled letters to form the surprise answer, as suggested by the above cartoon.

Print answer here

PUZZLE

106

JUMBLE®

Unscramble these four Jumbles, one letter to each square, to form four ordinary words.

WOLFN
ALFIL
TAHTCY
GIPELT
I'm glad we sent in double the amount we owe each month.
It's practically cut our mortgage length in half.
THEY DECIDED TO DOUBLE-UP ON THEIR MORTGAGE PAYMENTS, AND IT WAS ---

Now arrange the circled letters to form the surprise answer, as suggested by the above cartoon.

Print answer here

PUZZLE

107

JUMBLE®

Unscramble these four Jumbles, one letter to each square, to form four ordinary words.

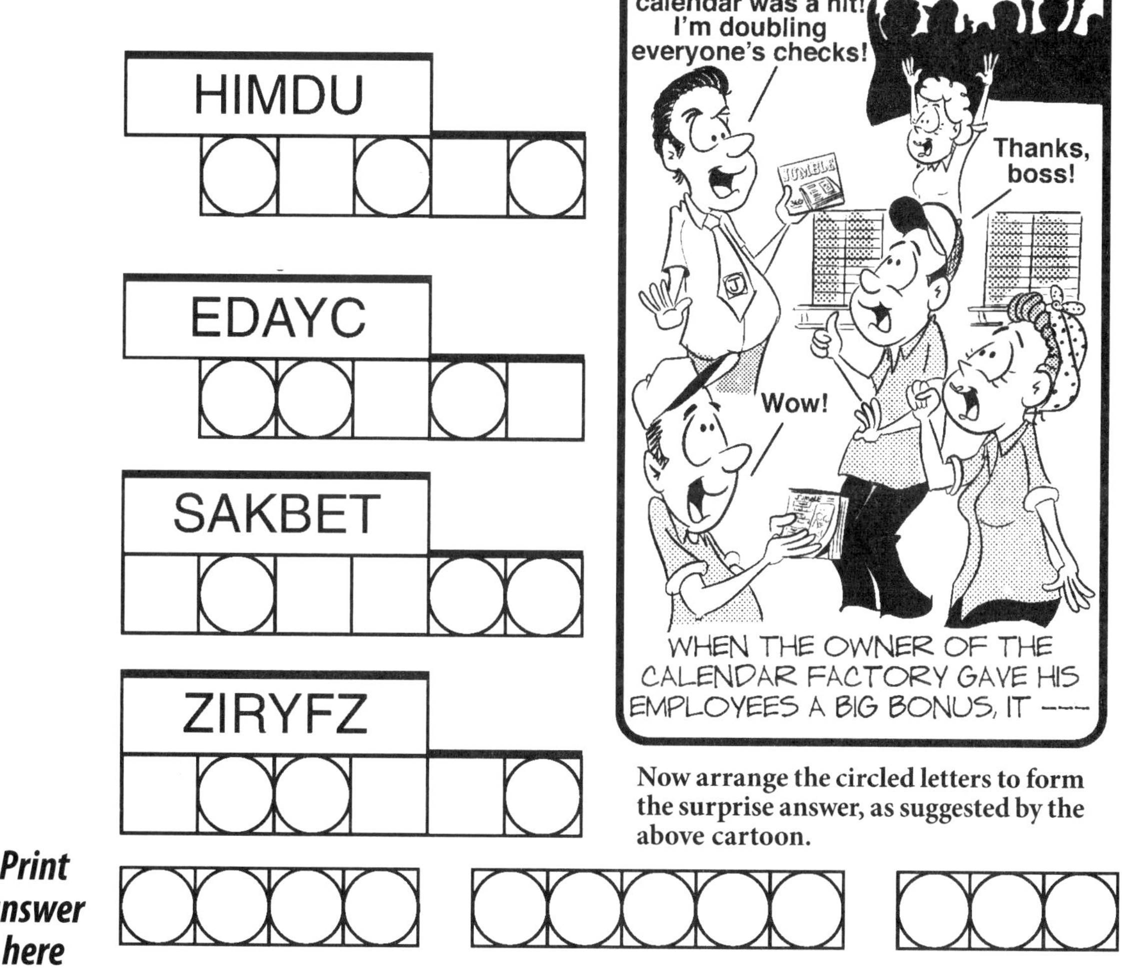
HIMDU
EDAYC
SAKBET
ZIRYFZ
The Jumble calendar was a hit! I'm doubling everyone's checks!
Thanks, boss!
Wow!
WHEN THE OWNER OF THE CALENDAR FACTORY GAVE HIS EMPLOYEES A BIG BONUS, IT ---

Now arrange the circled letters to form the surprise answer, as suggested by the above cartoon.

Print answer here

PUZZLE

108

JUMBLE®

Unscramble these four Jumbles, one letter to each square, to form four ordinary words.

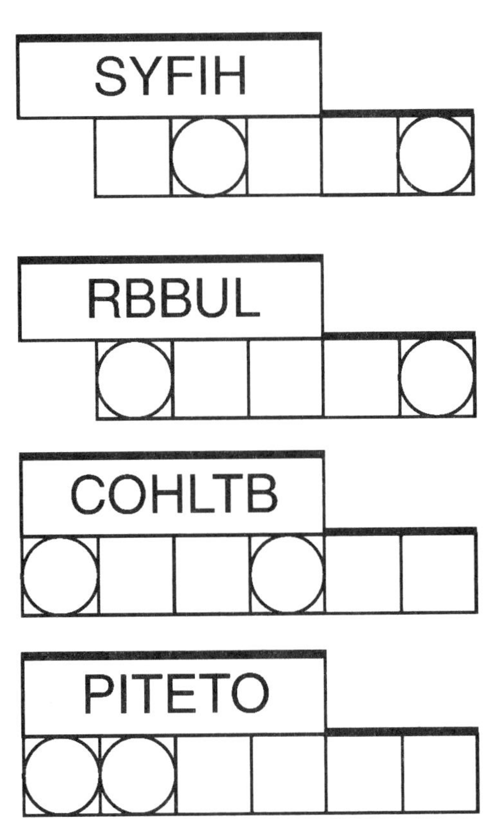

SYFIH
RBBUL
COHLTB
PITETO

Should I run to the hardware store for more?
It's too tough. They keep breaking.
DRILLING THROUGH THE HARD TILE WOULD BE DONE ---

Now arrange the circled letters to form the surprise answer, as suggested by the above cartoon.

Print answer here   

JUMBLE®

Unscramble these four Jumbles, one letter to each square, to form four ordinary words.

CLAKF
TTCAR
TUDIBO
CNADEN
You're not doing it right. Give it to me.
Why won't you open?
WHEN THE SQUIRREL COULDN'T GET THE WALNUT OPEN, HIS FRIEND WANTED ---

Now arrange the circled letters to form the surprise answer, as suggested by the above cartoon.

Print answer here

PUZZLE

110

JUMBLE®

Unscramble these four Jumbles, one letter to each square, to form four ordinary words.

IDYLO
SEASY
PILREP
UGPALE
Is the bunny hill too steep for you?
Are you trying to be funny?
WHEN HE STARTED MAKING FUN OF HIS WIFE'S SKIING ABILITY, HE WAS ON A ---

Now arrange the circled letters to form the surprise answer, as suggested by the above cartoon.

Print answer here

PUZZLE

111

JUMBLE®
Unscramble these four Jumbles, one letter to each square, to form four ordinary words.
SOGEO
CAHWT
ROHYTE
EERRBA
Farmer Jack's
My crops are selling so well, I need to expand.
Your produce is the best!
FARMER JA
WHEN THE FARMER BEGAN SELLING HIS OWN VEGGIES AND FRUITS, THE RESULT WAS A ---

Now arrange the circled letters to form the surprise answer, as suggested by the above cartoon.

Print answer here " - "

PUZZLE

112

JUMBLE®

Unscramble these four Jumbles, one letter to each square, to form four ordinary words.

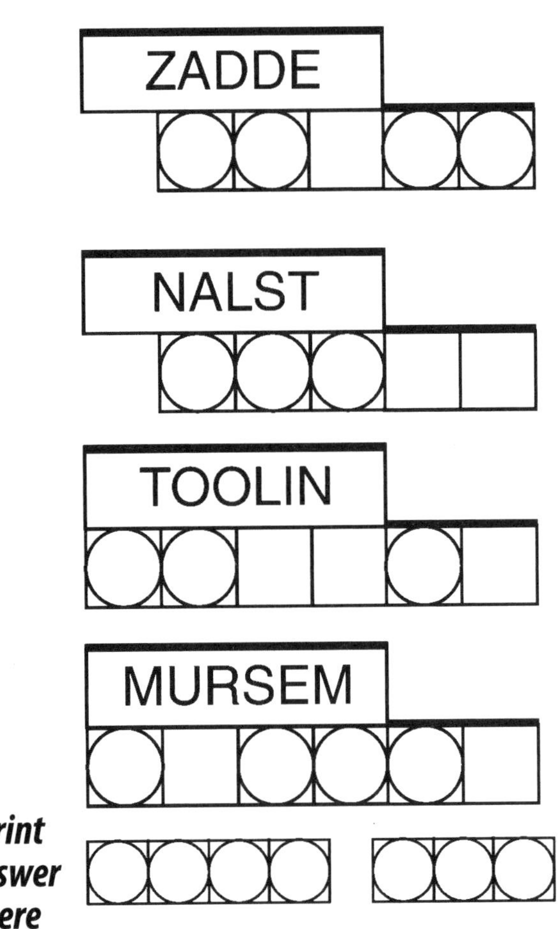

ZADDE
NALST
TOOLIN
MURSEM

Why aren't you two out celebrating your birthdays?
We've had plenty.
We'd rather play our weekly game.
THE TWINS TURNING 80 DIDN'T WANT A PARTY, JUST THE ---

Now arrange the circled letters to form the surprise answer, as suggested by the above cartoon.

Print answer here

JUMBLE®

Unscramble these four Jumbles, one letter to each square, to form four ordinary words.

FOLYT

FIWST

LOBDUE

SLOYGS

Now arrange the circled letters to form the surprise answer, as suggested by the above cartoon.

Print answer here

PUZZLE

114

JUMBLE®

Unscramble these four Jumbles, one letter to each square, to form four ordinary words.

TURMS
VOMIE
ICUTDN
NUNSEK
Are you going to buy that?
No. I'm almost finished.
Quick Reads
THE HISTORY OF FAT-FREE MILK
HISTORY OF FAT-FREE MILK
HISTORY OF FAT-FREE MILK
SHE PICKED A BOOK ON THE HISTORY OF FAT-FREE MILK AND ---

Now arrange the circled letters to form the surprise answer, as suggested by the above cartoon.

Print answer here

PUZZLE

115

JUMBLE®

Unscramble these four Jumbles, one letter to each square, to form four ordinary words.

GODUH
THACC
ROPURA
MURBEM
That Beatle, Pete Best, has a great name.
How about "Rich Sound" or "Snare Starkey"?
I'd like to go with "Ringo Starr."
WHEN HE CHOSE A STAGE NAME, RICHARD STARKEY CHOSE ONE THAT WASN'T ---

Now arrange the circled letters to form the surprise answer, as suggested by the above cartoon.

Print answer here

PUZZLE

116

JUMBLE®

Unscramble these four Jumbles, one letter to each square, to form four ordinary words.

HEWLE
ZAREC
TOTELU
RUYSEV
We've got you.
Uh-oh! Now I'm seeing double.
We get that a lot.
THE TWIN PARAMEDICS WERE ---

Now arrange the circled letters to form the surprise answer, as suggested by the above cartoon.

Print answer here " "

PUZZLE
117

JUMBLE®
Unscramble these four Jumbles, one letter to each square, to form four ordinary words.
RUCTO
TUPIN
SPAMYW
NULBED
You're all horrible at this. Rock the knife as I've shown or you fail.
WHEN TEACHING HER STUDENTS HOW TO CHOP GARLIC, THE CHEF DIDN'T ---
Now arrange the circled letters to form the surprise answer, as suggested by the above cartoon.
Print answer here

JUMBLE®

Unscramble these four Jumbles, one letter to each square, to form four ordinary words.

HYYLS
NILGF
MASOCI
GETWIH
You can see how quickly planes evolved.
1914
1953
1903
1937
IT ONLY TOOK ABOUT 50 YEARS TO GO FROM THE WRIGHT BROTHERS TO THE 707. ---

Now arrange the circled letters to form the surprise answer, as suggested by the above cartoon.

Print answer here

PUZZLE

119

JUMBLE®

Unscramble these four Jumbles, one letter to each square, to form four ordinary words.

PIRRO
OFREY
ANDNIL
MUBFEL
Yeah! Let's start cooking!
WHEN HE TRIED OUT THE BARBECUE GRILL HIS WIFE GOT HIM, HE WAS ---

Now arrange the circled letters to form the surprise answer, as suggested by the above cartoon.

Print answer here

JUMBLE®

Unscramble these four Jumbles, one letter to each square, to form four ordinary words.

STURB
KISYR
LENOYL
CEJERT
We can rest easy with the new agreement.
You guys are doing great work!
For sure.
THE PRISON GUARDS APPROVED THE NEW CONTRACT AND FELT THAT IT GAVE THEM ---

Now arrange the circled letters to form the surprise answer, as suggested by the above cartoon.

Print answer here

PUZZLE

121

JUMBLE®

Unscramble these four Jumbles, one letter to each square, to form four ordinary words.

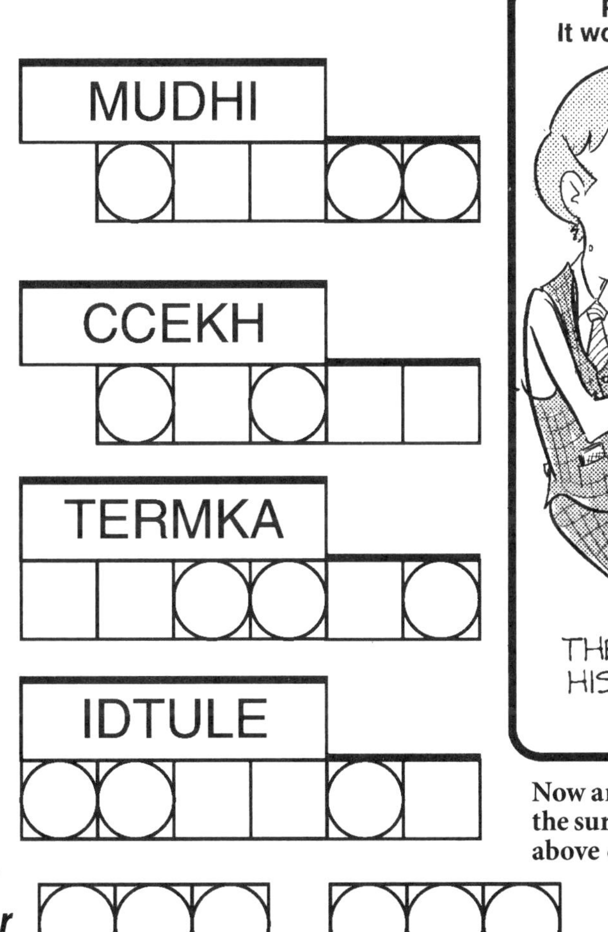
MUDHI
CCEKH
TERMKA
IDTULE

Phew!
It works now.
Mac King
Comedy Magic
Show
THE MAGICIAN REPAIRED HIS FAULTY PROP, AND FIXING IT ---

Now arrange the circled letters to form the surprise answer, as suggested by the above cartoon.

Print answer here

JUMBLE®

Unscramble these four Jumbles, one letter to each square, to form four ordinary words.

TOLAT

RHODC

PANIDU

HESBLU

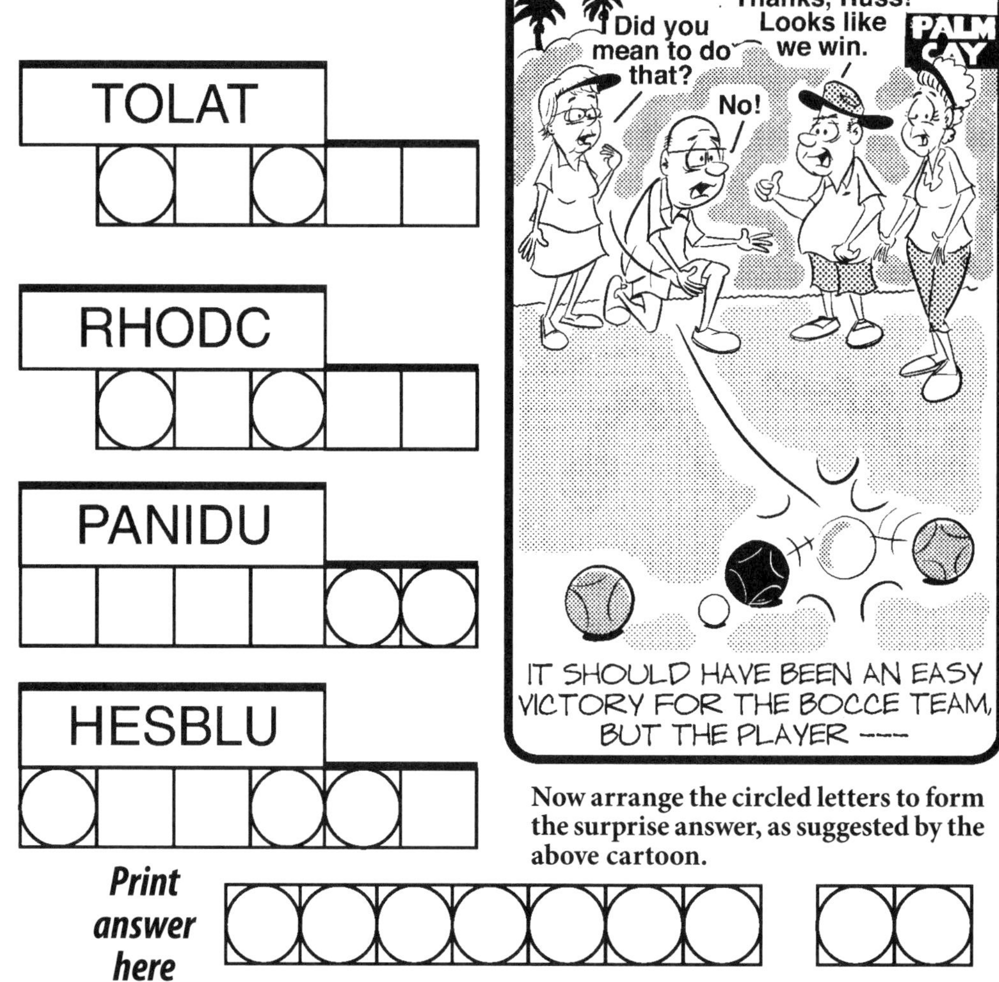
Did you mean to do that?
No!
Thanks, Russ! Looks like we win.
PALM CAY
IT SHOULD HAVE BEEN AN EASY VICTORY FOR THE BOCCE TEAM, BUT THE PLAYER ----

Now arrange the circled letters to form the surprise answer, as suggested by the above cartoon.

Print answer here

PUZZLE

123

JUMBLE®

Unscramble these four Jumbles, one letter to each square, to form four ordinary words.

GITAN
OYPUS
WRAPLS
NUTEBA
So, how do you like it?
No one makes better armor.
THE MEDIEVAL TAILOR CREATED ARMORED OUTFITS FOR KNIGHTS. IT WAS HIS ---

Now arrange the circled letters to form the surprise answer, as suggested by the above cartoon.

Print answer here

PUZZLE

124

JUMBLE®

Unscramble these four Jumbles, one letter to each square, to form four ordinary words.

CUPOH

NITLF

SOOCSM

CURDEE

If you don't remove this wet snow, you'll never get re-elected.
I'll have to dip into my backup cash.
MAYOR
HE NEEDED TO PAY SOMEONE TO SHOVEL THE MELTING SNOW. LUCKILY, HE HAD A ---

Now arrange the circled letters to form the surprise answer, as suggested by the above cartoon.

Print answer here

PUZZLE

125

JUMBLE®

Unscramble these four Jumbles, one letter to each square, to form four ordinary words.

SRUNP
SEMYS
GRACIL
GADEAN
He has made us so much better.
Now I can hit the high notes.
Follow me.
THE CHURCH'S NEW CHOIR DIRECTOR WAS WELL LIKED. MEMBERS OF THE CHOIR ----
Print answer here
HIS

Now arrange the circled letters to form the surprise answer, as suggested by the above cartoon.

JUMBLE®

Unscramble these four Jumbles, one letter to each square, to form four ordinary words.

CIPYK

ROGPU

SMULSE

MENOYK

Now arrange the circled letters to form the surprise answer, as suggested by the above cartoon.

Print answer here

PUZZLE

127

JUMBLE®

Unscramble these four Jumbles, one letter to each square, to form four ordinary words.

HNOYE
NUYNB
COTKEL
COSLIA
Wow! Nothing gets past him.
He loves playing.
THE DOG WHO WAS VERY GOOD AT PLAYING FETCH WAS ---

Now arrange the circled letters to form the surprise answer, as suggested by the above cartoon.

Print answer here

PUZZLE

128

JUMBLE®

Unscramble these four Jumbles, one letter to each square, to form four ordinary words.

WROGL
TIDRH
GRLAUF
VFARLO
Can you two scare up any more room for some more candy?
I'm stuffed.
AFTER EATING SO MUCH CANDY, THE SCARY-LOOKING TRICK-OR-TREATERS WERE ---

Now arrange the circled letters to form the surprise answer, as suggested by the above cartoon.

Print answer here “ ◯◯◯◯◯◯ - ◯◯◯◯ ”

JUMBLE®

Unscramble these four Jumbles, one letter to each square, to form four ordinary words.

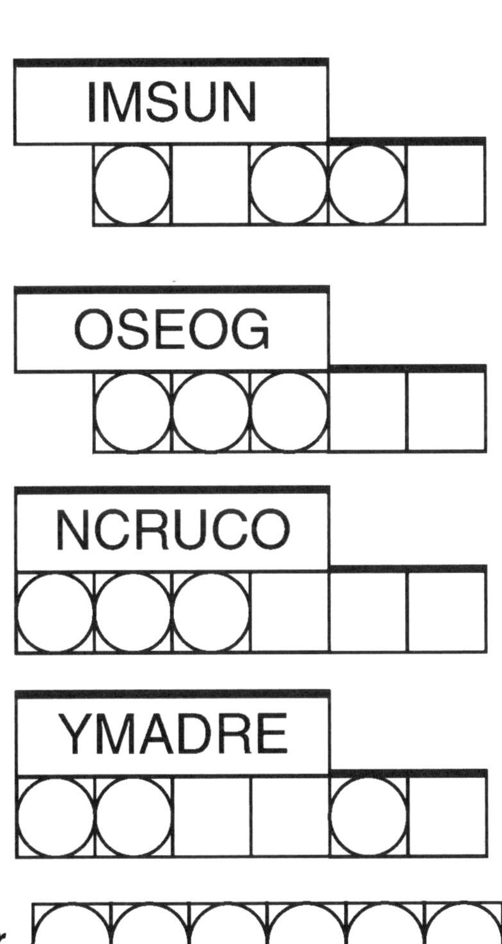
IMSUN
OSEOG
NCRUCO
YMADRE

This land would be perfect to grow trees, plants and more.
20 Acres FOR SALE
What if we put our differences aside and bought it together?
THE PLANT-NURSERY OWNERS WERE COMPETITORS UNTIL THEY FOUND SOME ----

Now arrange the circled letters to form the surprise answer, as suggested by the above cartoon.

Print answer here

JUMBLE®

Unscramble these four Jumbles, one letter to each square, to form four ordinary words.

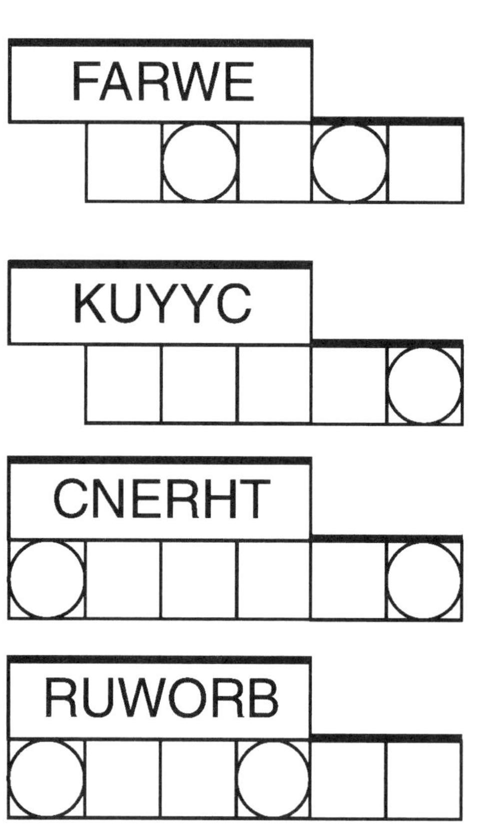

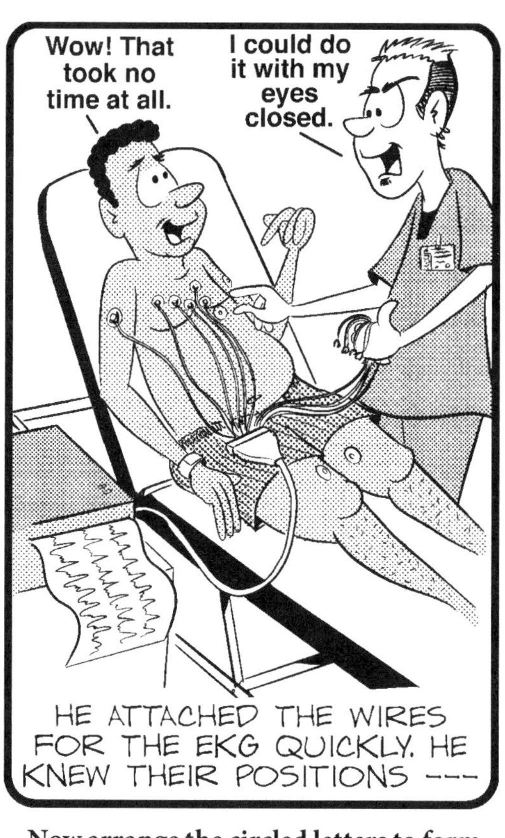

Now arrange the circled letters to form the surprise answer, as suggested by the above cartoon.

Print answer here  

PUZZLE

131

JUMBLE®

Unscramble these four Jumbles, one letter to each square, to form four ordinary words.

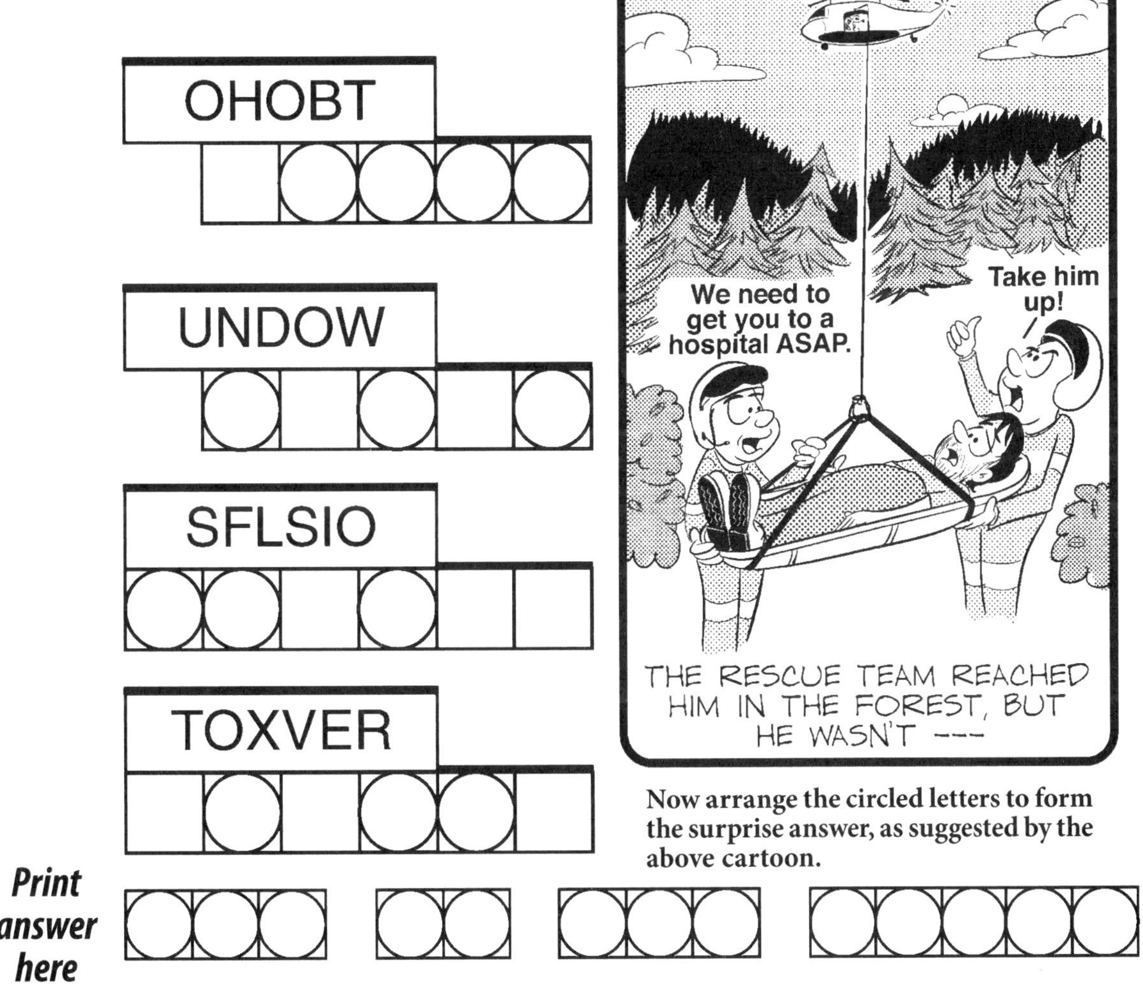
OHOBT
UNDOW
SFLSIO
TOXVER
We need to get you to a hospital ASAP.
Take him up!
THE RESCUE TEAM REACHED HIM IN THE FOREST, BUT HE WASN'T ---

Now arrange the circled letters to form the surprise answer, as suggested by the above cartoon.

Print answer here

JUMBLE®

Unscramble these four Jumbles, one letter to each square, to form four ordinary words.

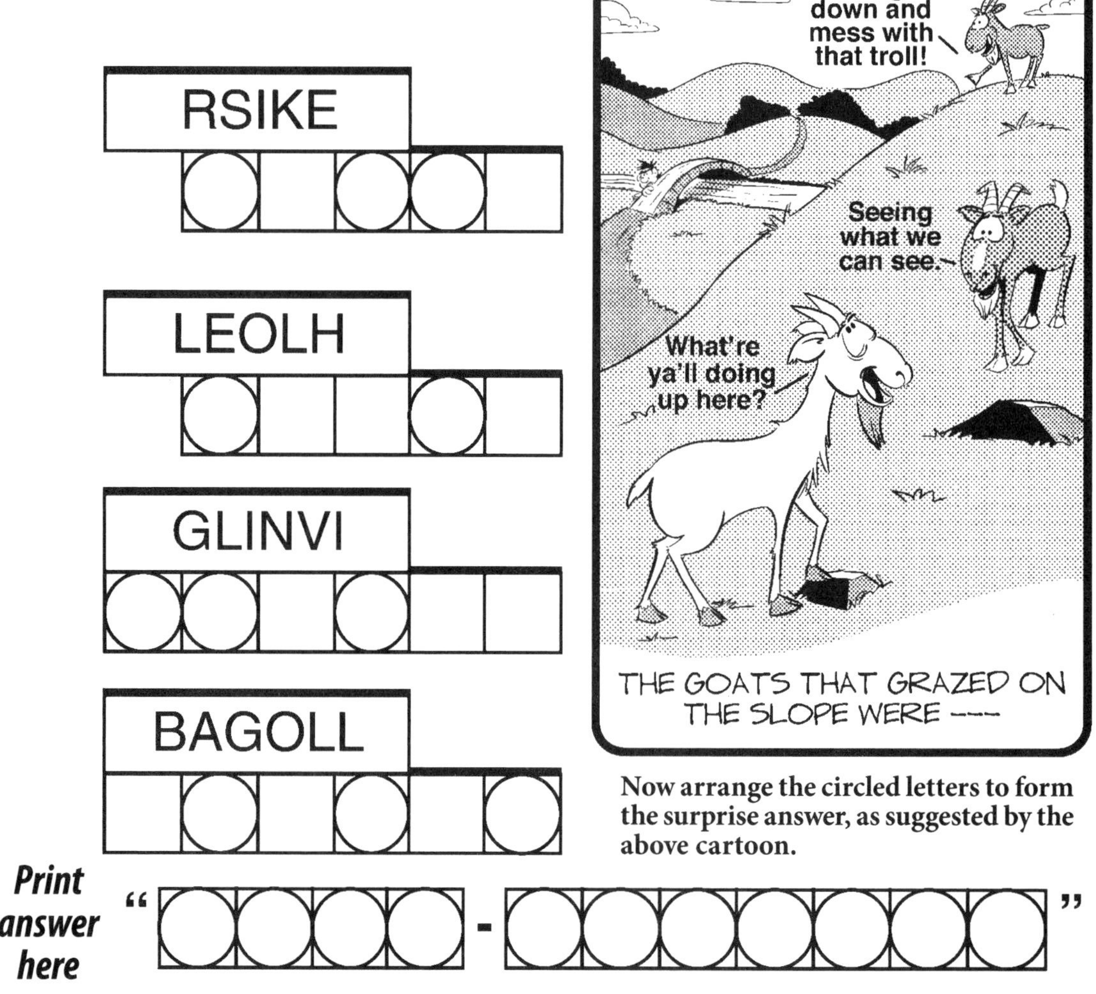
RSIKE
LEOLH
GLINVI
BAGOLL
Let's go down and mess with that troll!
Seeing what we can see.
What're ya'll doing up here?
THE GOATS THAT GRAZED ON THE SLOPE WERE ---

Now arrange the circled letters to form the surprise answer, as suggested by the above cartoon.

Print answer here " ◯◯◯◯ - ◯◯◯◯◯◯◯ "

JUMBLE®

Unscramble these four Jumbles, one letter to each square, to form four ordinary words.

PHECR

BLAFE

RASPIN

VIRTHE

She almost didn't come.
We pulled it off.
Wow! What a surprise.
This is from me.
TO RECEIVE HER GIFTS IN PERSON, SHE NEEDED TO ---

Now arrange the circled letters to form the surprise answer, as suggested by the above cartoon.

Print answer here

JUMBLE®

Unscramble these four Jumbles, one letter to each square, to form four ordinary words.

WEYRA
NOGGI
SORETE
DLUPED
BLOWING IN THE WIND ENERGY CORP.
HERE COMES THE SUN ENERGY CORP.
You're going down!
We're the future, you blow-hard.
THE COMPETITION BETWEEN THE ENERGY COMPANIES WAS A ---

Now arrange the circled letters to form the surprise answer, as suggested by the above cartoon.

Print answer here

PUZZLE

135

JUMBLE®

Unscramble these four Jumbles, one letter to each square, to form four ordinary words.

NEGIS
LNAFK
TCLOHB
LUNFAT
These are just as good as Kona.
We rejected these last month.
HE TOLD THEM THAT HE GREW GREAT COFFEE, BUT HE WAS ---

Now arrange the circled letters to form the surprise answer, as suggested by the above cartoon.

Print answer here

PUZZLE

136

JUMBLE®

Unscramble these four Jumbles, one letter to each square, to form four ordinary words.

UNDOH

DALGE

KTREMA

PNNIKA

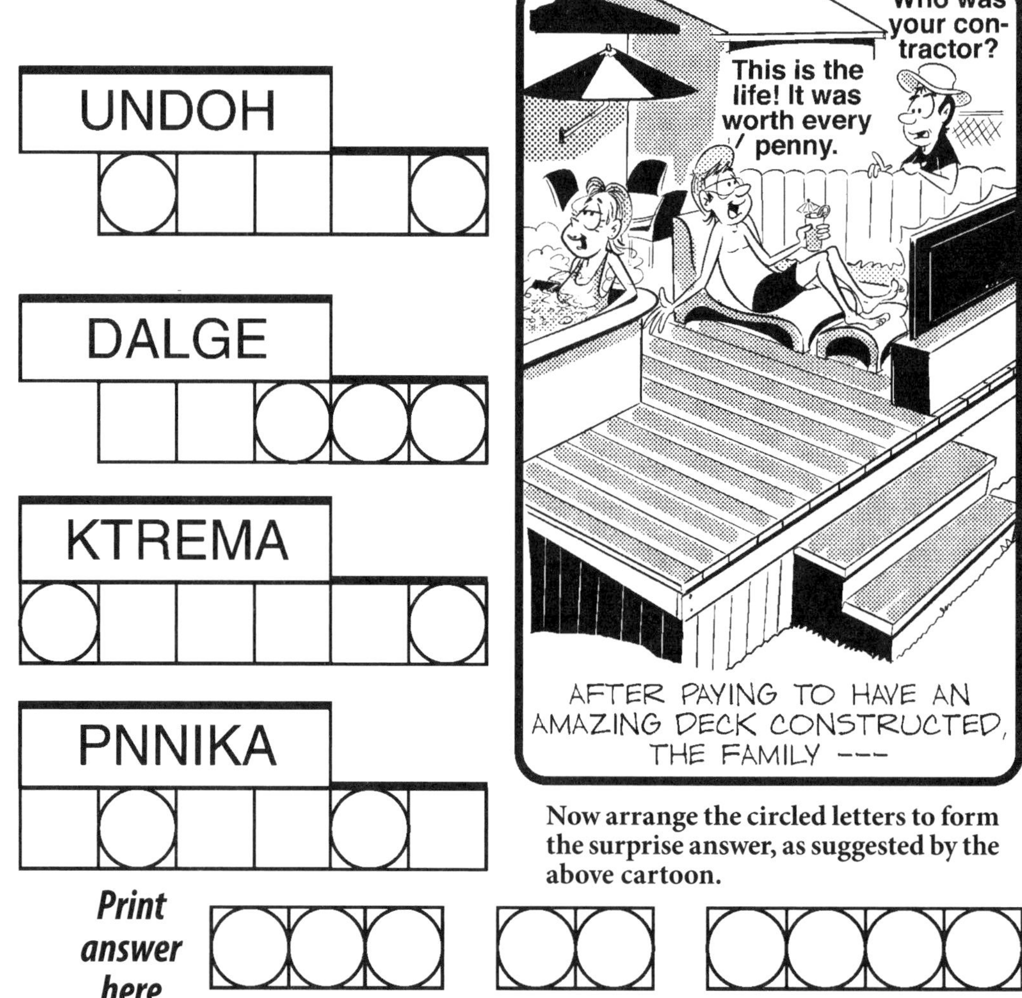

Who was your con-tractor?
This is the life! It was worth every penny.
AFTER PAYING TO HAVE AN AMAZING DECK CONSTRUCTED, THE FAMILY ---

Now arrange the circled letters to form the surprise answer, as suggested by the above cartoon.

Print answer here

PUZZLE

137

JUMBLE®

Unscramble these four Jumbles, one letter to each square, to form four ordinary words.

CARTK
CATHH
WRANOR
DEMLOU
What do you say we listen to some of your music while we throw this saucer?
He's so cute!
You are all right, dude!
You like dogs, too?
THE HUMANS FOUND THE ALIENS TO BE VERY SENSIBLE AND ---

Now arrange the circled letters to form the surprise answer, as suggested by the above cartoon.

Print answer here

JUMBLE®

Unscramble these four Jumbles, one letter to each square, to form four ordinary words.

LRUBB

GRAWE

KUICPP

PLATEL

Billy said we weren't getting snacks after the game!
Oh, brother.
WHEN THE YOUNG PLAYERS STARTED CRYING, THE BASEBALL FIELD BECAME A ---

Now arrange the circled letters to form the surprise answer, as suggested by the above cartoon.

Print answer here " ◯◯◯◯ " ◯◯◯◯

JUMBLE®

Unscramble these four Jumbles, one letter to each square, to form four ordinary words.

LEWLD
CIHKT
HECCNA
RIOMRR
Today's Guest JUMBLER is
JOE STATON
Artist for DICK TRACY
CALLING DICK TRACY! GREAT JOB SOLVING THE LAST CASE. GET HERE ASAP. WE HAVE A NEW CASE FOR YOU.
THE CITY WAS SAFER BECAUSE OF DICK TRACY'S ---
Now arrange the circled letters to form the surprise answer, as suggested by the above cartoon.

Print answer here

JUMBLE®

Unscramble these four Jumbles, one letter to each square, to form four ordinary words.

ZAPAL
PYMET
LIMENG
CAZDIO
Today's Guest JUMBLER is
BILL MORRISON
Creator of ROSWELL, Little Green Man
THE LITTLE GREEN MAN FROM OUTER SPACE FELT ALONE AND ---
Print answer here

Now arrange the circled letters to form the surprise answer, as suggested by the above cartoon.

JUMBLE®

Unscramble these four Jumbles, one letter to each square, to form four ordinary words.

Today's Guest JUMBLER is
GREG CRAVENS
Creator of The BUCKETS
WHAT'S THE BEST WAY TO DISPLAY A *BACKWARD* DRAWING?

ARNGD

PEWIR

MEELAF

RWHYOT

Now arrange the circled letters to form the surprise answer, as suggested by the above cartoon.

Print answer here IN A

PUZZLE

142

JUMBLE®

Unscramble these four Jumbles, one letter to each square, to form four ordinary words.

OVPIT
MUPEL
CHDNER
GTELIP
Today's Guest JUMBLER is
JASON CHATFIELD
Artist for GINGER MEGGS
WHAT'D YA GIVE HIM?!
AFTER GINGER GAVE THE KANGAROO A COFFEE, HE WAS ---
Print answer here

Now arrange the circled letters to form the surprise answer, as suggested by the above cartoon.

PUZZLE

143

JUMBLE®

Unscramble these four Jumbles, one letter to each square, to form four ordinary words.

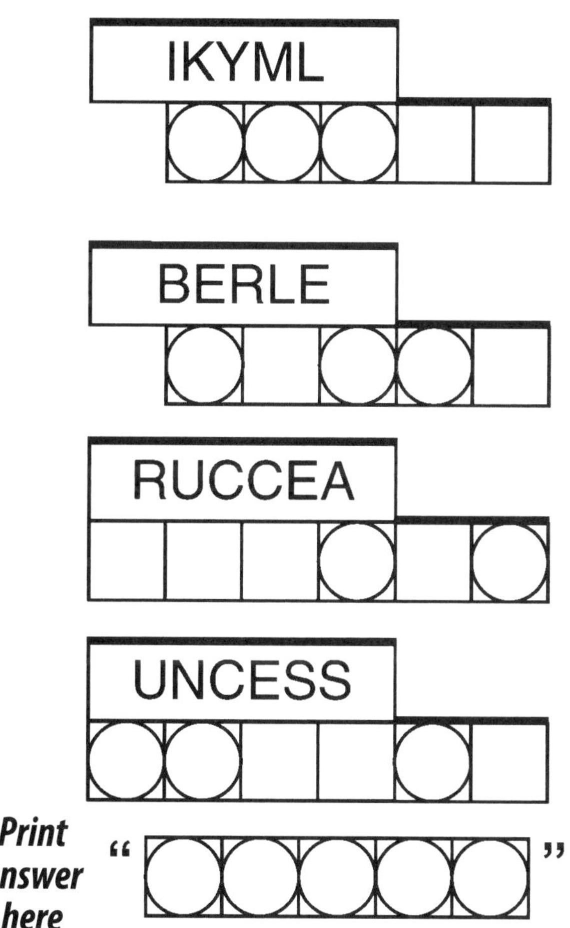

Now arrange the circled letters to form the surprise answer, as suggested by the above cartoon.

Print answer here " "

PUZZLE

144

JUMBLE®

Unscramble these four Jumbles, one letter to each square, to form four ordinary words.

COLEL

SRIOV

REEFTR

WUDINN

Today's Guest JUMBLER is
Mason Mastroianni
B.C. Cartoonist
IT LOOKS NICE, BUT WHAT'S IT DO?
HOW SHOULD I KNOW?
THOR'S INVENTIONS
WHEN THOR INVENTED THE WHEEL, HE STARTED A ---

Now arrange the circled letters to form the surprise answer, as suggested by the above cartoon.

Print answer here

JUMBLE®

Unscramble these four Jumbles, one letter to each square, to form four ordinary words.

VIRRE
ZELGA
MYIKPS
TREEJS

I'm glad we woke up when we did.
I'm glad we didn't go to bed late last night.
THE HOT AIR BALLOONISTS WERE ABLE TO SEE THE SUN COME UP BECAUSE THEY WERE ---

Now arrange the circled letters to form the surprise answer, as suggested by the above cartoon.

Print answer here

PUZZLE

146

JUMBLE®

Unscramble these four Jumbles, one letter to each square, to form four ordinary words.

DOYDL

CENIE

SKEORM

BUTEAP

I've analyzed your dilemma and have concluded that I can only charge you the minimum.
Thank you!
SHERLOCK HOLMES GAVE HIS FRIENDS DISCOUNTS, AND THEY WERE THANKFUL FOR HIS ---

Now arrange the circled letters to form the surprise answer, as suggested by the above cartoon.

Print answer here

PUZZLE

147

JUMBLE®

Unscramble these four Jumbles, one letter to each square, to form four ordinary words.

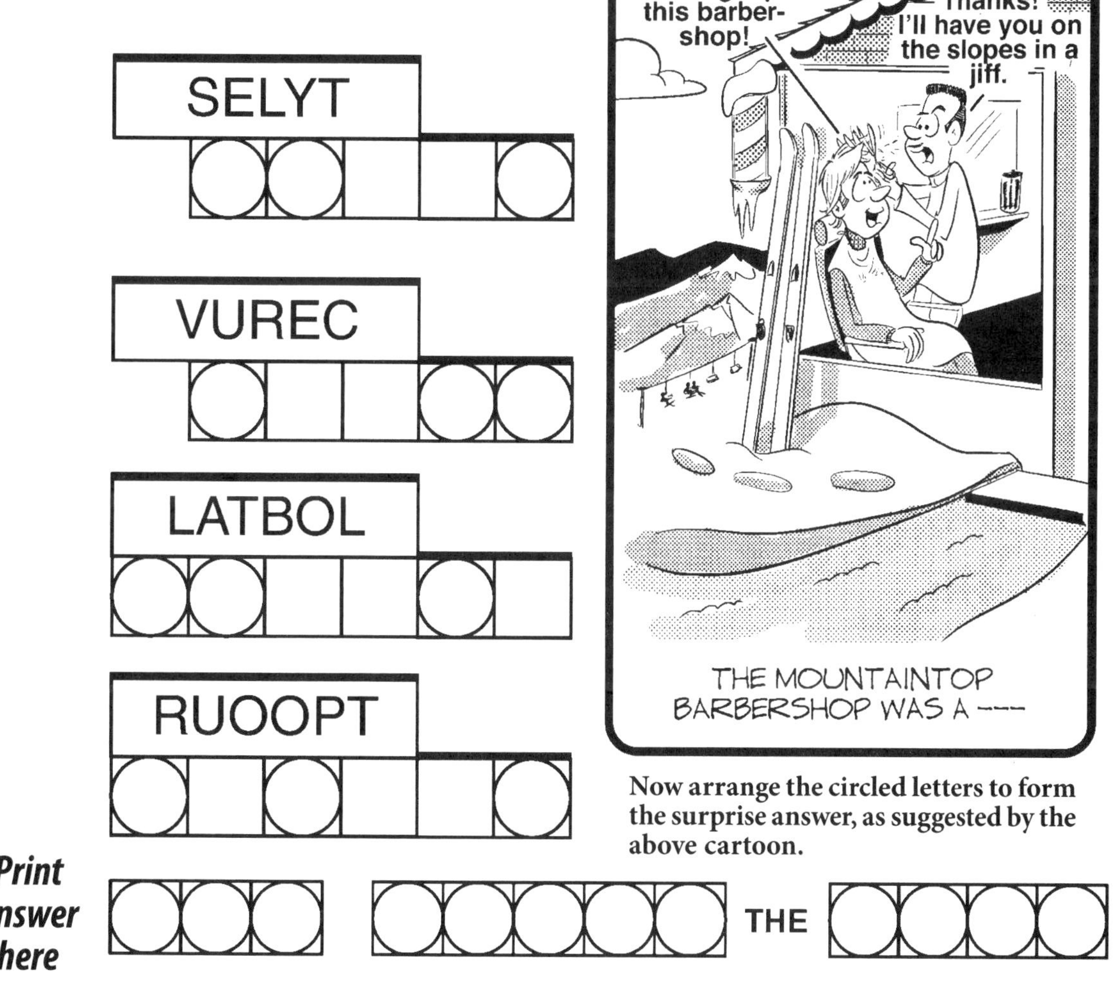
SELYT
VUREC
LATBOL
RUOOPT
Nothing tops this barber-shop!
Thanks! I'll have you on the slopes in a jiff.
THE MOUNTAINTOP BARBERSHOP WAS A ---

Now arrange the circled letters to form the surprise answer, as suggested by the above cartoon.

Print answer here ◯◯◯ ◯◯◯◯◯ THE ◯◯◯◯

PUZZLE

148

JUMBLE®

Unscramble these four Jumbles, one letter to each square, to form four ordinary words.

NAYHD
GTIMH
NURSEU
PONCAY
Ready for a glass of wine?
Let me put this in the oven. Then I'm going to clean up and watch the game.
AFTER RUBBING THE SEASONING ON THE THANKSGIVING TURKEY, SHE HAD ---

Now arrange the circled letters to form the surprise answer, as suggested by the above cartoon.

Print answer here " ◯◯◯◯◯ " ◯◯ HER ◯◯◯◯◯

PUZZLE

149

JUMBLE®

Unscramble these four Jumbles, one letter to each square, to form four ordinary words.

CANTE
URSIV
WLEFLO
VARCOT
They just keep going.
The wind on the North Sea is as renewable as it gets.
THE SEA-BASED WIND FARM PRODUCED THIS TYPE OF ENERGY ---

Now arrange the circled letters to form the surprise answer, as suggested by the above cartoon.

Print answer here "◯◯◯-◯◯◯◯-◯◯◯◯◯"

PUZZLE

150

JUMBLE®

Unscramble these four Jumbles, one letter to each square, to form four ordinary words.

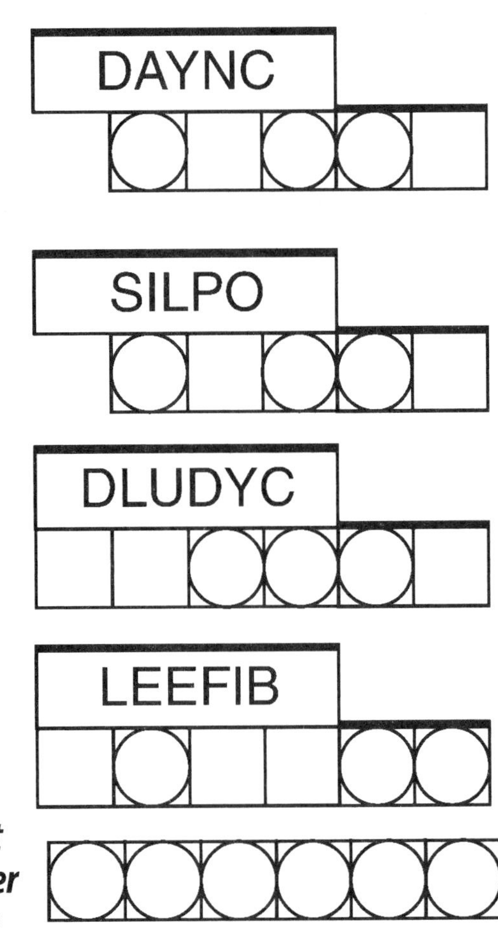

DAYNC
SILPO
DLUDYC
LEEFIB

It's not your night.
Why doesn't she ever take the day off?
THE SYMPHONY'S BACKUP VIOLINIST DIDN'T LIKE PLAYING ---

Now arrange the circled letters to form the surprise answer, as suggested by the above cartoon.

Print answer here

PUZZLE

151

JUMBLE®

Unscramble these four Jumbles, one letter to each square, to form four ordinary words.

MORGO

NYACF

EZENSE

ROYHTN

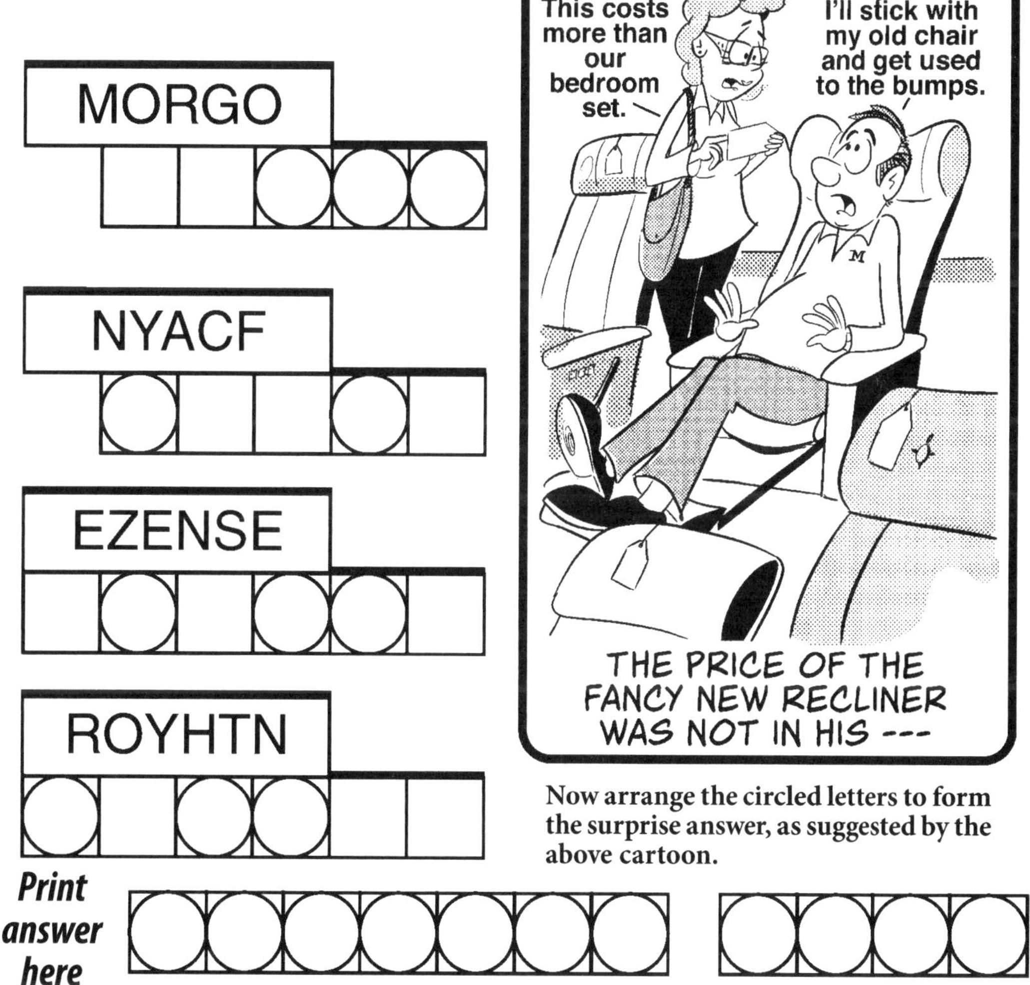

Whoa! This costs more than our bedroom set.
Really? I think I'll stick with my old chair and get used to the bumps.
M
THE PRICE OF THE FANCY NEW RECLINER WAS NOT IN HIS ---

Now arrange the circled letters to form the surprise answer, as suggested by the above cartoon.

Print answer here

PUZZLE

152

JUMBLE®

Unscramble these four Jumbles, one letter to each square, to form four ordinary words.

SIYFH

EARPO

LNEATG

PARSNI

Hey! That's the second bull's-eye it bounced out of.
You should just give up.
THE TIPS OF THE DARTS WERE DULL, SO THROWING THEM AT THE DARTBOARD WAS ---

Now arrange the circled letters to form the surprise answer, as suggested by the above cartoon.

Print answer here

PUZZLE

153

JUMBLE®

Unscramble these four Jumbles, one letter to each square, to form four ordinary words.

POMET
KAWET
MOLANS
KELPIC
Everyone will get a turn.
Wow!
Me next!
WHEN TELESCOPES WERE INVENTED, PEOPLE WERE EXCITED TO ---

Now arrange the circled letters to form the surprise answer, as suggested by the above cartoon.

Print answer here

JUMBLE®

Unscramble these four Jumbles, one letter to each square, to form four ordinary words.

HNARC
DARTY
UQEAPO
OVENKI
Ready to go in, Rusty?
WELCOME
WHEN THE LITTLE BOY ARRIVED AT THE GATES OF THE AMUSEMENT PARK, HE WAS ---

Now arrange the circled letters to form the surprise answer, as suggested by the above cartoon.

Print answer here

JUMBLE®

Unscramble these four Jumbles, one letter to each square, to form four ordinary words.

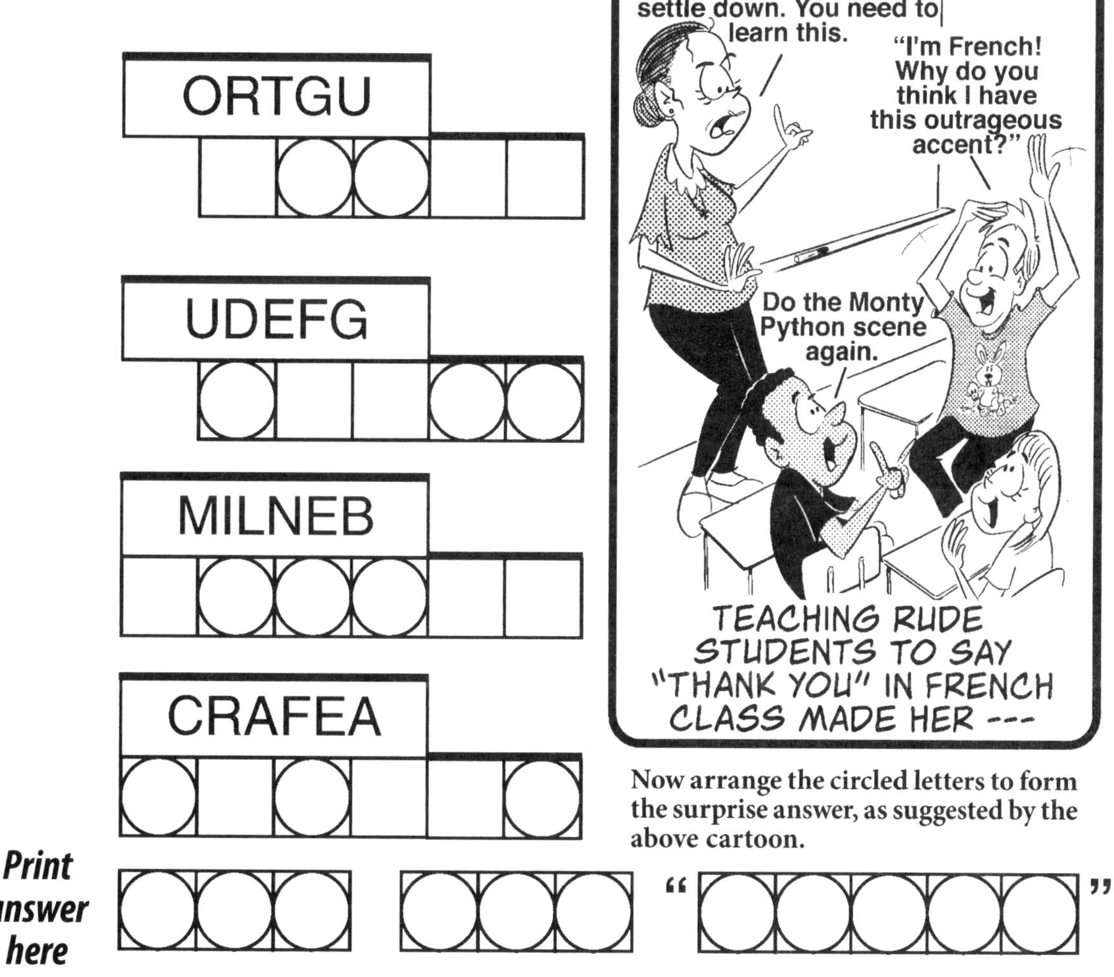
ORTGU
UDEFG
MILNEB
CRAFEA
Please, please, please settle down. You need to learn this.
"I'm French! Why do you think I have this outrageous accent?"
Do the Monty Python scene again.
TEACHING RUDE STUDENTS TO SAY "THANK YOU" IN FRENCH CLASS MADE HER ---

Now arrange the circled letters to form the surprise answer, as suggested by the above cartoon.

Print answer here

JUMBLE®

Unscramble these four Jumbles, one letter to each square, to form four ordinary words.

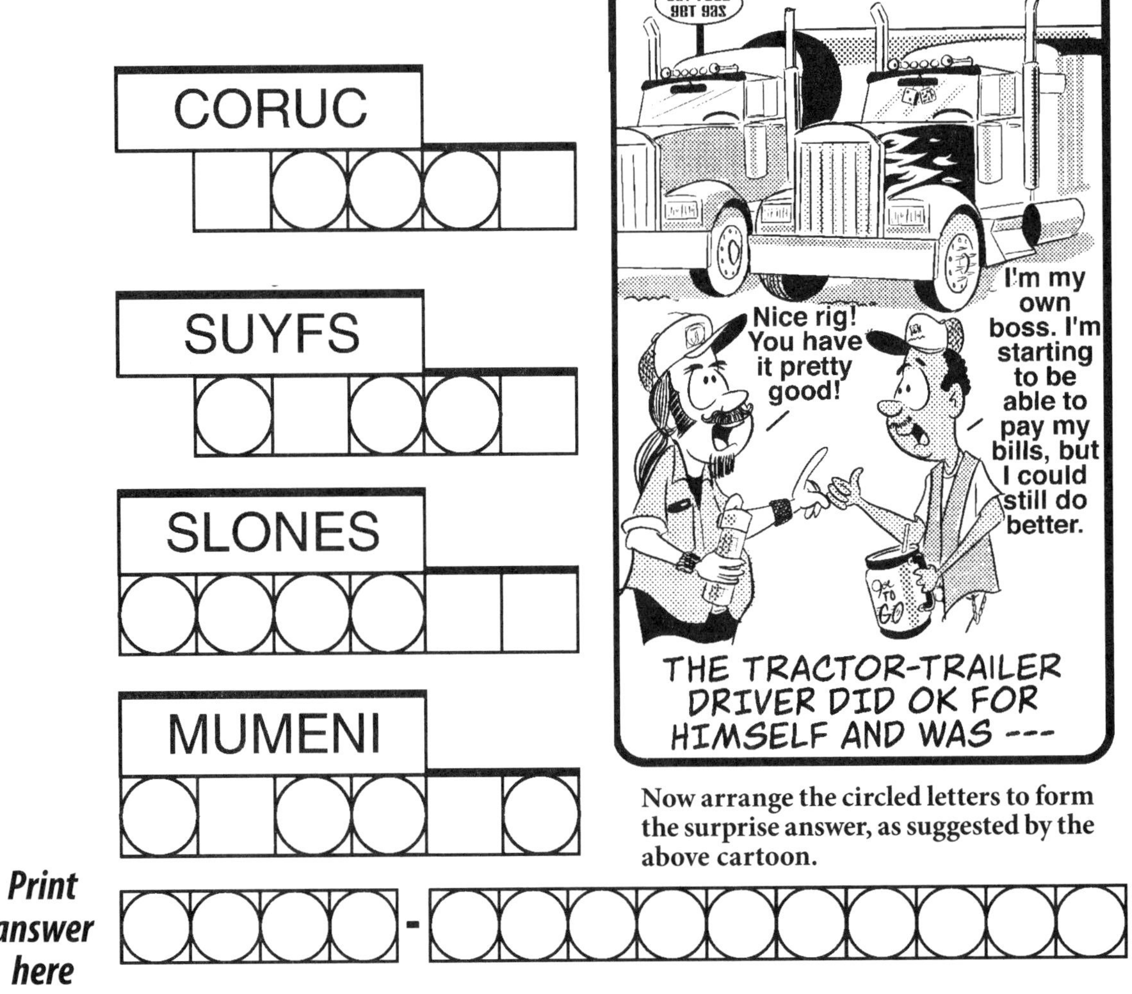
CORUC
SUYFS
SLONES
MUMENI
EAT FOOD
GET GAS
Nice rig! You have it pretty good!
I'm my own boss. I'm starting to be able to pay my bills, but I could still do better.
THE TRACTOR-TRAILER DRIVER DID OK FOR HIMSELF AND WAS ---

Now arrange the circled letters to form the surprise answer, as suggested by the above cartoon.

Print answer here

PUZZLE

157

JUMBLE®
Unscramble these four Jumbles, one letter to each square, to form four ordinary words.
TDPAA
TOBUA
HOYTER
SPULCT
Hang in there.
Here's another one.
You saved the day!
WHEN FIREFIGHTERS RESCUED THE KITTENS FROM A TREE, THEY AVERTED A ---

Now arrange the circled letters to form the surprise answer, as suggested by the above cartoon.

Print answer here "◯◯◯-◯◯◯◯◯◯◯◯"

PUZZLE

158

JUMBLE®

Unscramble these four Jumbles, one letter to each square, to form four ordinary words.

LUTYR

TIODT

GOIBNX

NEETTX

So, shirts get hung up instead of putting them in the basket. Agreed?
Yes. I agree.
AFTER THEY ARGUED ABOUT THE WRINKLED CLOTHES, THEIR PROBLEMS WERE ---

Now arrange the circled letters to form the surprise answer, as suggested by the above cartoon.

Print answer here

PUZZLE

159

JUMBLE®

Unscramble these four Jumbles, one letter to each square, to form four ordinary words.

GAMIE
ANLCA
NKYSNI
DIRHEN
I'm trying.
You'll need to get over to take the next right.
AFTER LEARNING THAT THEIR REGULAR BOWLING ALLEY WAS CLOSED, THEY ---

Now arrange the circled letters to form the surprise answer, as suggested by the above cartoon.

Print answer here

JUMBLE®

Unscramble these four Jumbles, one letter to each square, to form four ordinary words.

OLOGI

HNAKT

PRILTE

SCNAVA

Now arrange the circled letters to form the surprise answer, as suggested by the above cartoon.

Print answer here

JUMBLE®

Cuisine

Challenger Puzzles

JUMBLE®

Unscramble these six Jumbles, one letter to each square, to form six ordinary words.

ENSCOD

GURFEE

SOWDRY

REDAIM

YULNOH

TESKAB

WHAT COLOR DID HE PAINT THE SUN AND THE WIND?

Now arrange the circled letters to form the surprise answer, as suggested by the above cartoon.

Print answer here

THE ☐☐☐ ☐☐☐☐, THE ☐☐☐☐☐ ☐☐☐☐

JUMBLE®

Unscramble these six Jumbles, one letter to each square, to form six ordinary words.

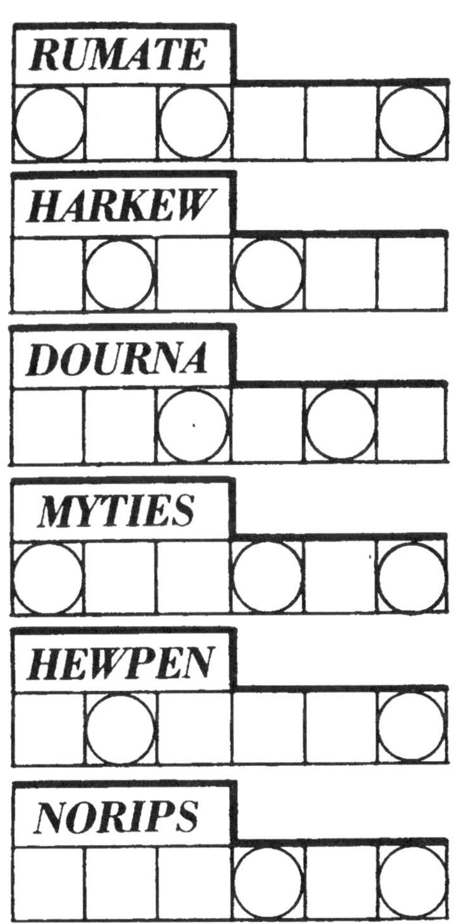

Now arrange the circled letters to form the surprise answer, as suggested by the above cartoon.

Print answer here

JUMBLE®

Unscramble these six Jumbles, one letter to each square, to form six ordinary words.

LARCIA

HAPNOR

DINCIT

GEEREM

GLAUPE

YOLFEN

Now arrange the circled letters to form the surprise answer, as suggested by the above cartoon.

Print answer here

JUMBLE®

Unscramble these six Jumbles, one letter to each square, to form six ordinary words.

Now arrange the circled letters to form the surprise answer, as suggested by the above cartoon.

Print answer here

PUZZLE

165

JUMBLE®

Unscramble these six Jumbles, one letter to each square, to form six ordinary words.

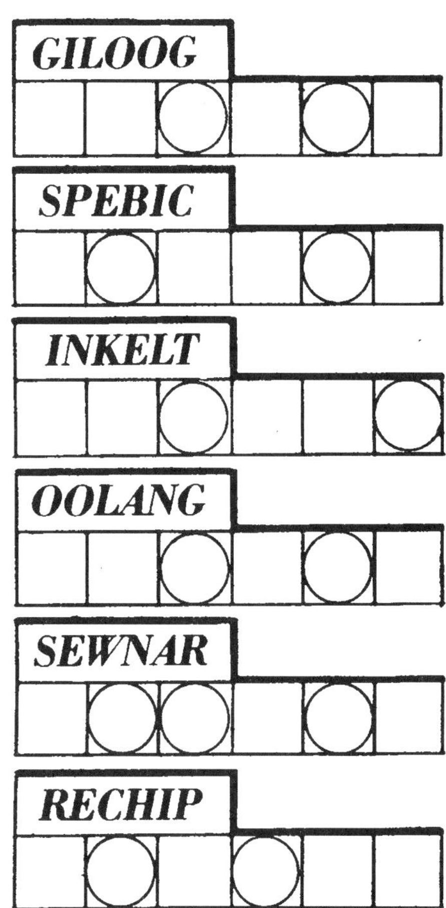
GILOOG
SPEBIC
INKELT
OOLANG
SEWNAR
RECHIP

WHAT THEY MIGHT SPEAK IN LONDON'S TRAFALGAR SQUARE.

Now arrange the circled letters to form the surprise answer, as suggested by the above cartoon.

Print answer here

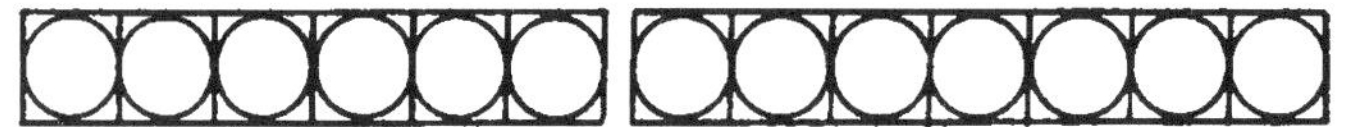

JUMBLE®

Unscramble these six Jumbles, one letter to each square, to form six ordinary words.

TYMARR
CLOIPY
MORNIF
YAMBIG
CLINOU
DUNBOA
Wow! That should reduce the cost of living!
WHAT GEORGE WASHINGTON MADE.

Now arrange the circled letters to form the surprise answer, as suggested by the above cartoon.

Print answer here

A ◯◯◯◯◯◯ ◯◯ ◯◯◯

PUZZLE

167

JUMBLE®

Unscramble these six Jumbles, one letter to each square, to form six ordinary words.

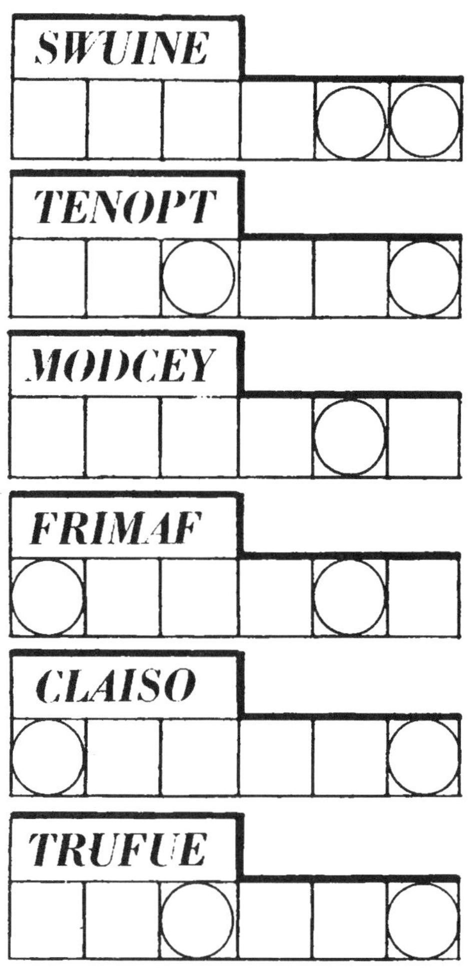
SWUINE
TENOPT
MODCEY
FRIMAF
CLAISO
TRUFUE

WHAT HE SAID WHEN THE JUDGE INFORMED HIM THAT HE'D BEEN BROUGHT BEFORE THE COURT FOR DRINKING.

Now arrange the circled letters to form the surprise answer, as suggested by the above cartoon.

Print answer here

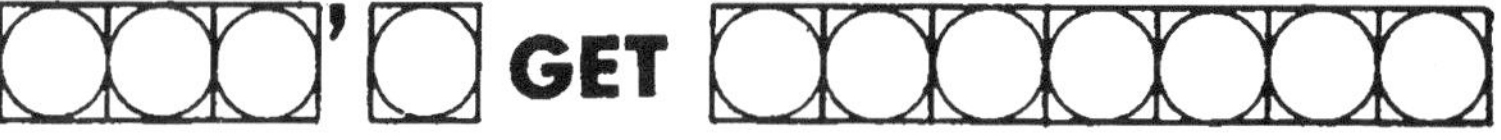
GET

PUZZLE

168

JUMBLE®

Unscramble these six Jumbles, one letter to each square, to form six ordinary words.

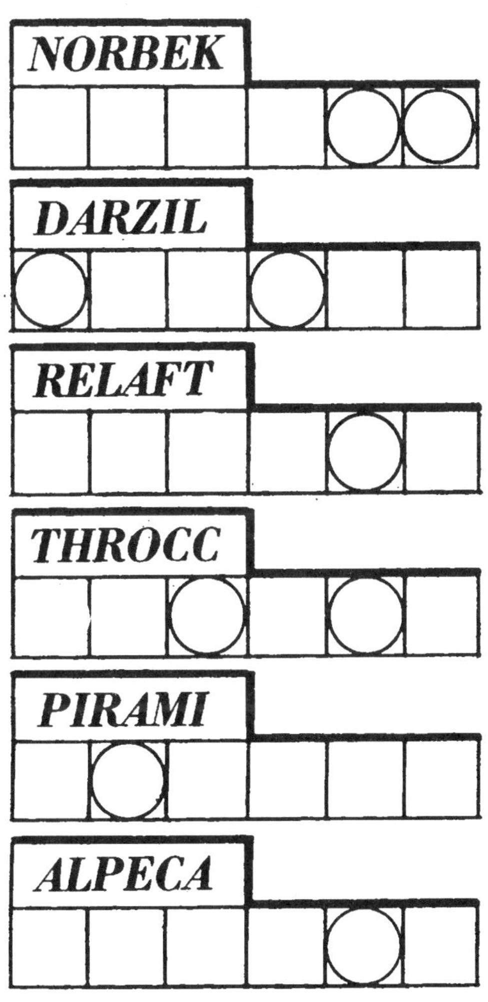

Now arrange the circled letters to form the surprise answer, as suggested by the above cartoon.

Print answer here

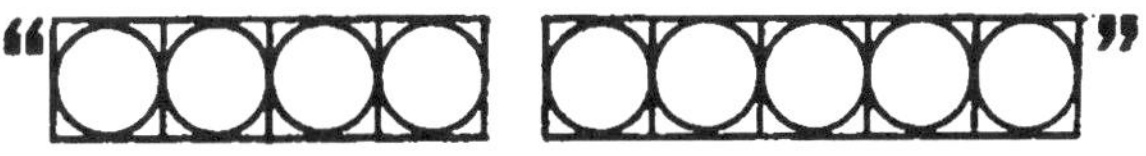

PUZZLE

169

JUMBLE®

Unscramble these six Jumbles, one letter to each square, to form six ordinary words.

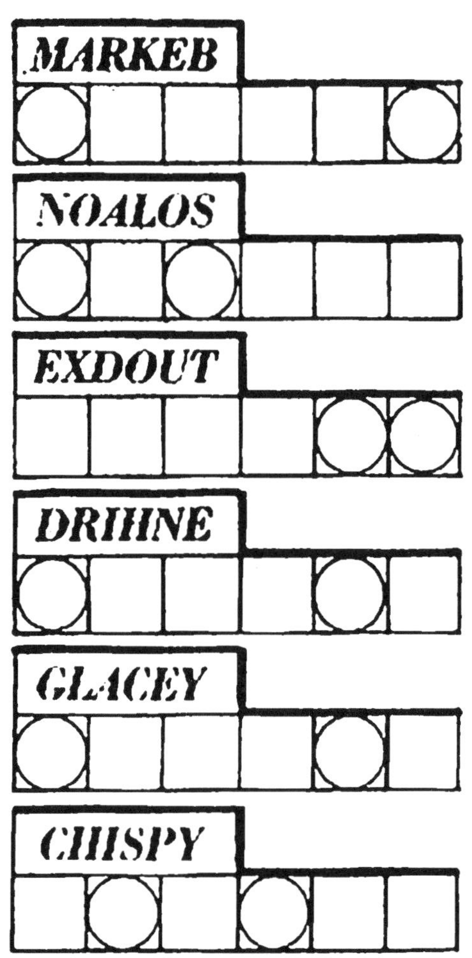

Now arrange the circled letters to form the surprise answer, as suggested by the above cartoon.

Print answer here

"◯◯◯◯◯◯" ◯◯◯◯◯◯◯◯

PUZZLE 170

JUMBLE®

Unscramble these six Jumbles, one letter to each square, to form six ordinary words.

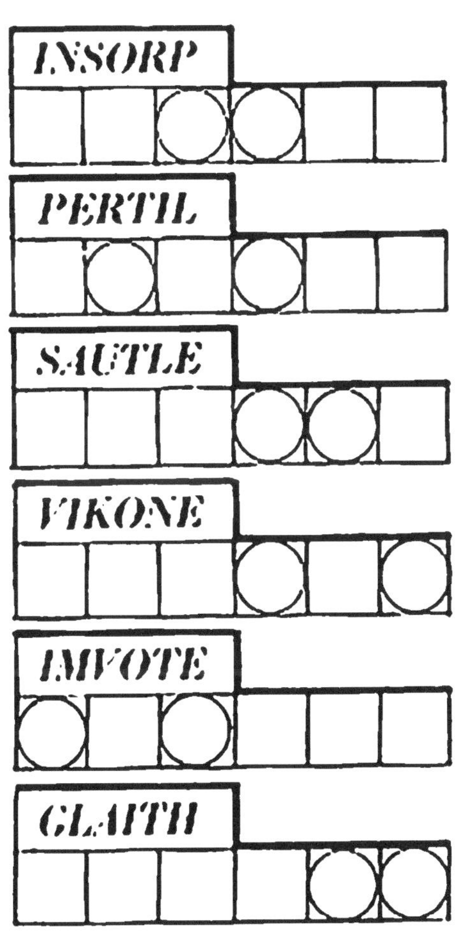

Now arrange the circled letters to form the surprise answer, as suggested by the above cartoon.

Print answer here

PUZZLE

171

JUMBLE®

Unscramble these six Jumbles, one letter to each square, to form six ordinary words.

HOYTER

NZEEES

THOSEO

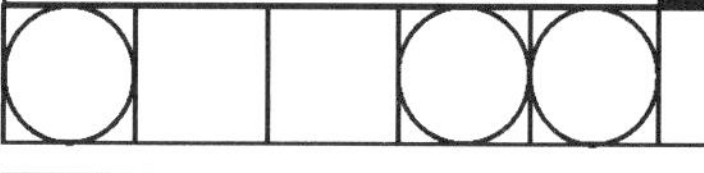
DEMPIE

AGETOE

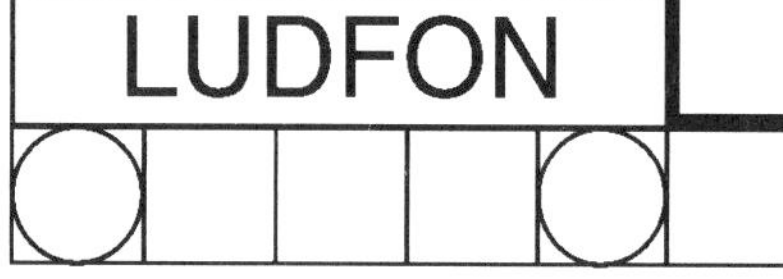
LUDFON

Follow me online and I'll keep you updated on these storms all day.
SUNDAY
Strong Storms
I can update everyone, just fine.
I feel a heat wave coming on.

THE EVENING WEATHERMAN WAS WORRIED THAT THE NEW METEOROLOGIST WOULD ---

Now arrange the circled letters to form the surprise answer, as suggested by the above cartoon.

Print answer here

JUMBLE®

Unscramble these six Jumbles, one letter to each square, to form six ordinary words.

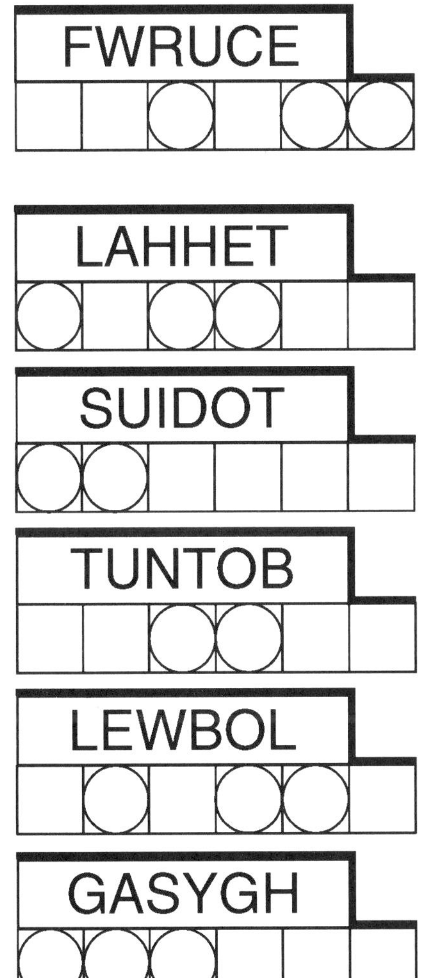
FWRUCE
LAHHET
SUIDOT
TUNTOB
LEWBOL
GASYGH

We'll miss her. Agatha was an amazing author.
Hear, hear.
I can't believe there will be no more stories from her.
WHEN AGATHA CHRISTIE'S FUNERAL SERVICE WAS OVER, THEY SAID ---

Now arrange the circled letters to form the surprise answer, as suggested by the above cartoon.

Print answer here

JUMBLE®

Unscramble these six Jumbles, one letter to each square, to form six ordinary words.

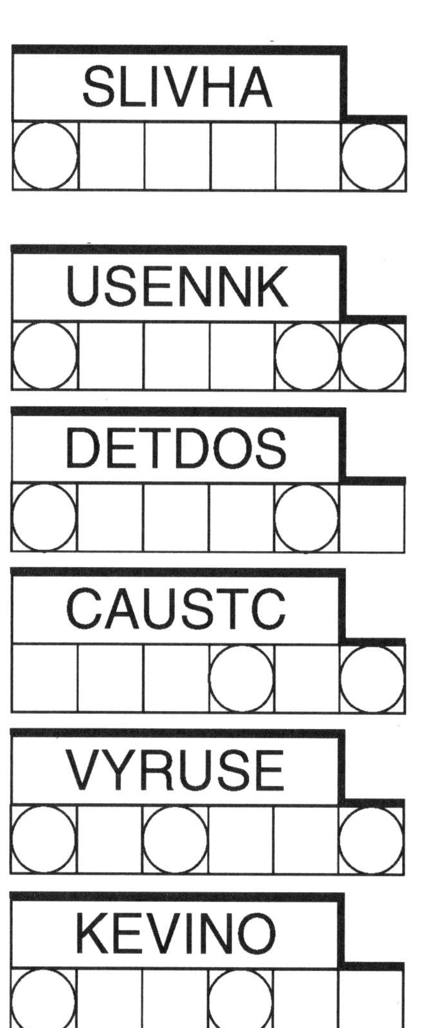
SLIVHA
USENNK
DETDOS
CAUSTC
VYRUSE
KEVINO

I was born in Tuskegee. When I was four, we moved to Mobile. I loved playing baseball when I was your age.
They sure love learning about him.
Where did you go to school?
Did you have any pets?
THE RETIRED TEACHER LOVED GIVING THE GRANDKIDS A ---

Now arrange the circled letters to form the surprise answer, as suggested by the above cartoon.

Print answer here

" - "

PUZZLE

174

JUMBLE®

Unscramble these six Jumbles, one letter to each square, to form six ordinary words.

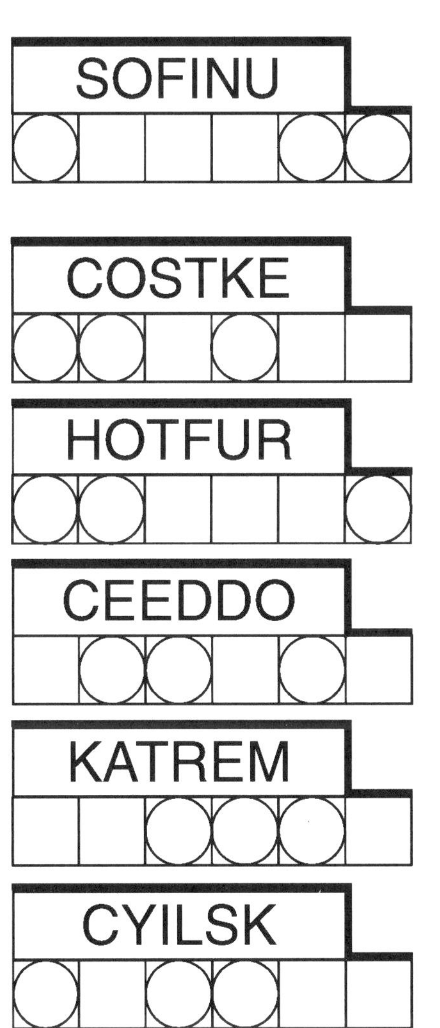

SOFINU
COSTKE
HOTFUR
CEEDDO
KATREM
CYILSK

Wow! Those look amazing on you!
I love these! I'll take them!
SHE LOVED THE NEW DESIGNER SANDALS. ONE PAIR IN PARTICULAR ---

Now arrange the circled letters to form the surprise answer, as suggested by the above cartoon.

Print answer here

JUMBLE®

Unscramble these six Jumbles, one letter to each square, to form six ordinary words.

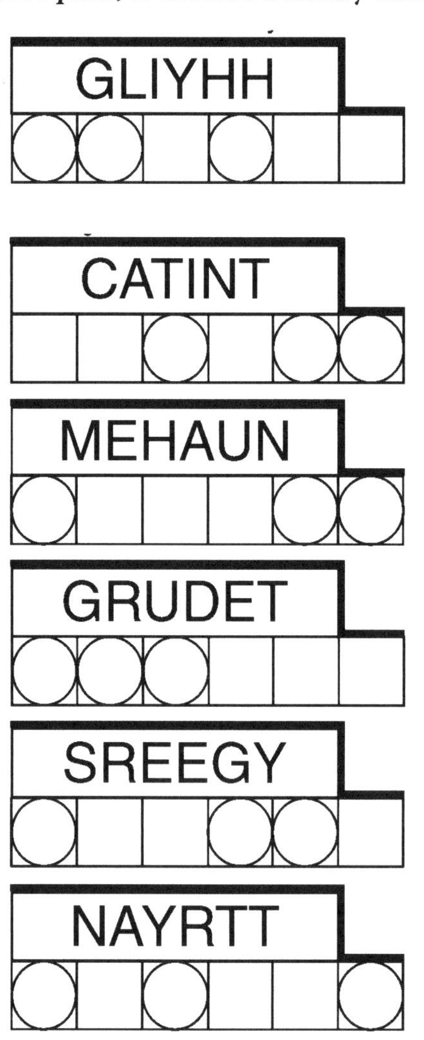
GLIYHH
CATINT
MEHAUN
GRUDET
SREEGY
NAYRTT

Look, honey! I can't believe it still fits!
Of course it does, honey. Why wouldn't it?
SHE SAID THAT HER WEDDING DRESS STILL FIT, BUT SHE WAS ---

Now arrange the circled letters to form the surprise answer, as suggested by the above cartoon.

Print answer here

PUZZLE

176

JUMBLE®

Unscramble these six Jumbles, one letter to each square, to form six ordinary words.

USEARS

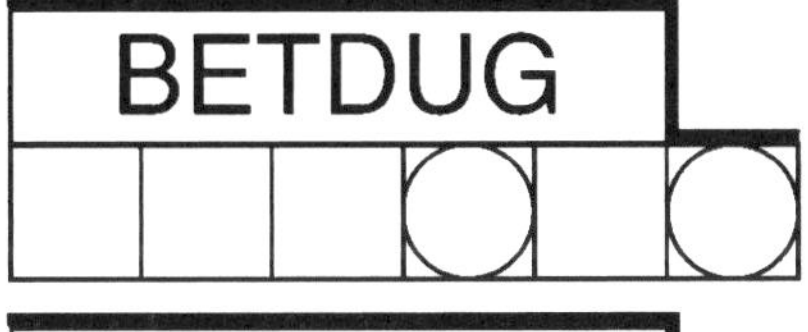
BETDUG

GRUFIE

VEVIER

LERONL

ODLONE

I think she's the one. She's really got me pumped up.
It looks like things are working out for you two.
THE BODYBUILDER KNEW HE WAS IN LOVE AFTER EXPERIENCING ---

Now arrange the circled letters to form the surprise answer, as suggested by the above cartoon.

Print answer here

JUMBLE®

Unscramble these six Jumbles, one letter to each square, to form six ordinary words.

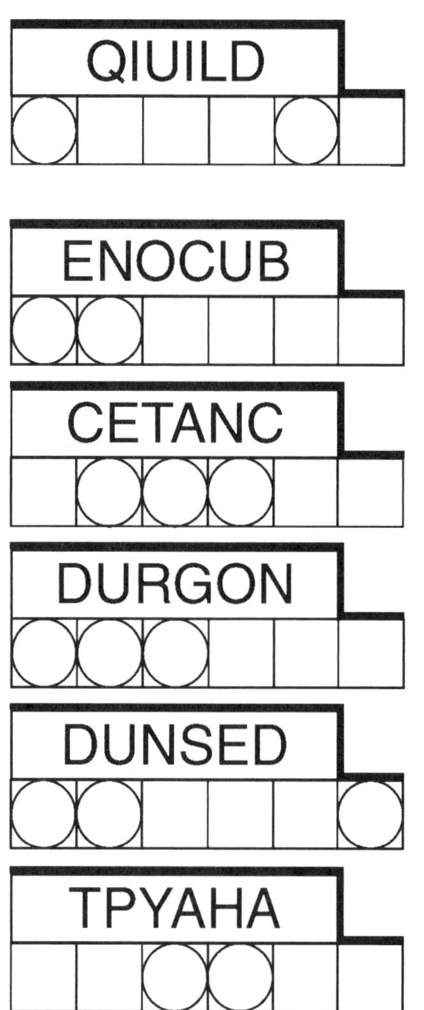
QIUILD
ENOCUB
CETANC
DURGON
DUNSED
TPYAHA

I knew it! Don't you even think about lighting that up.
But it's a Cuban.
HE PROMISED TO QUIT, SO WHEN HIS WIFE CAUGHT HIM ABOUT TO SMOKE A STOGIE, IT WAS ---

Now arrange the circled letters to form the surprise answer, as suggested by the above cartoon.

Print answer here

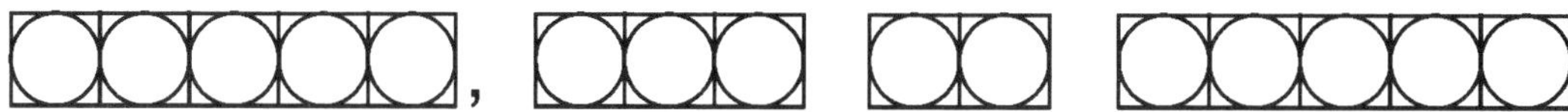

PUZZLE

178

JUMBLE®

Unscramble these six Jumbles, one letter to each square, to form six ordinary words.

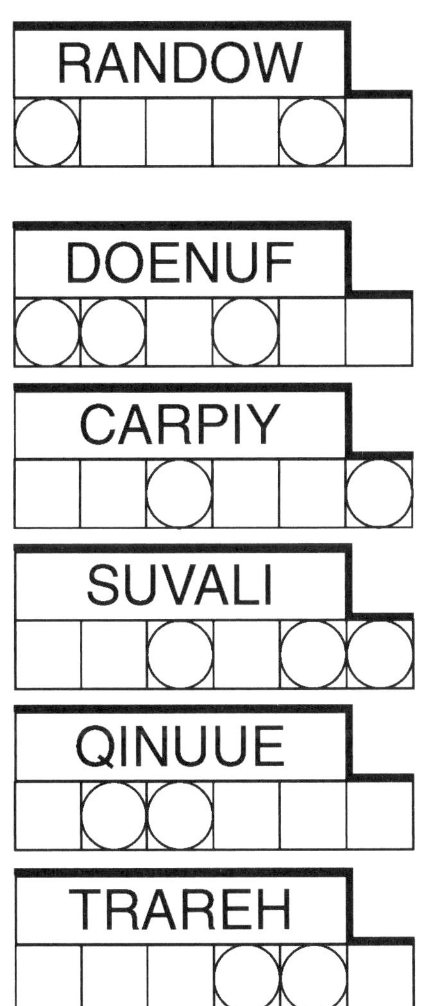

RANDOW
DOENUF
CARPIY
SUVALI
QINUUE
TRAREH

the sydney collection
She always gets the best models.
Her summer line is so organized.
THE MODELS WALKED DOWN THE RUNWAY IN AN ---

Now arrange the circled letters to form the surprise answer, as suggested by the above cartoon.

Print answer here

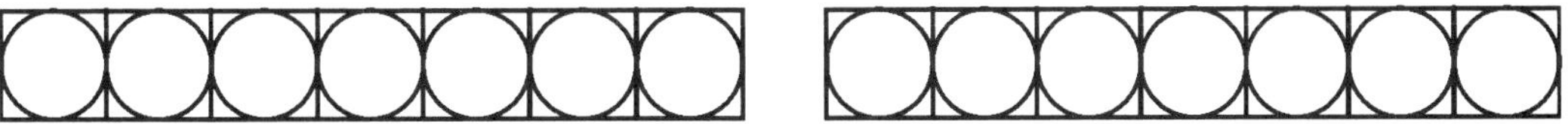

JUMBLE®

Unscramble these six Jumbles, one letter to each square, to form six ordinary words.

NORFIM

CUGOLN

CRACES

PCOYUC

Now arrange the circled letters to form the surprise answer, as suggested by the above cartoon.

Print answer here

PUZZLE

180

JUMBLE®

Unscramble these six Jumbles, one letter to each square, to form six ordinary words.

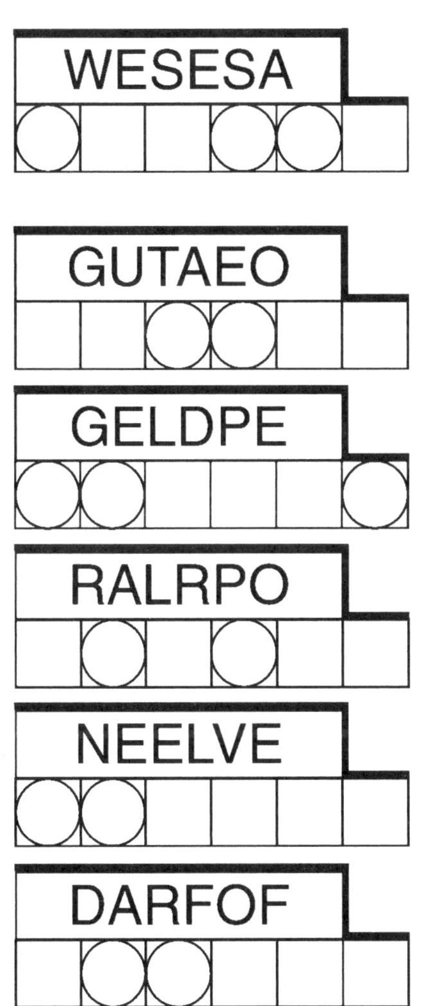

WESESA
GUTAEO
GELDPE
RALRPO
NEELVE
DARFOF

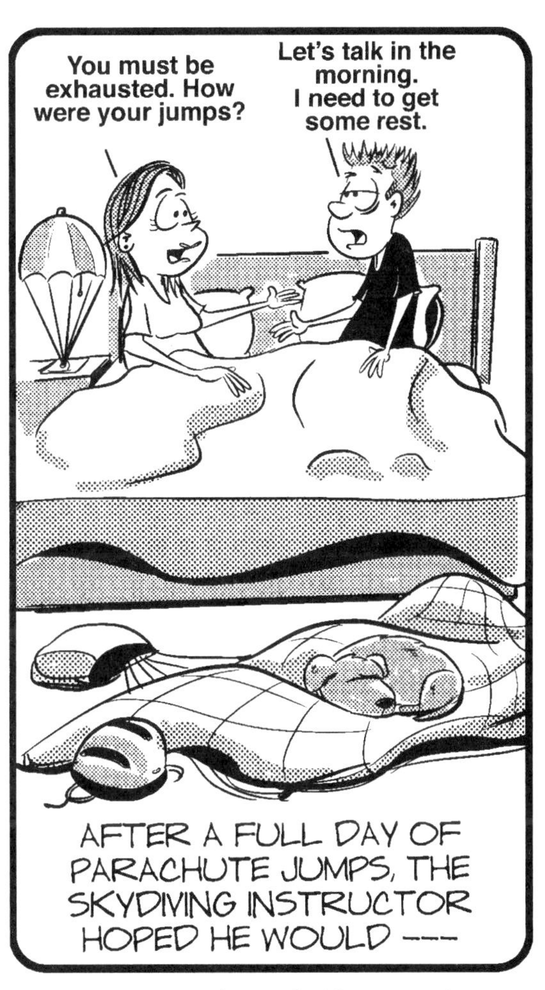

You must be exhausted. How were your jumps?
Let's talk in the morning. I need to get some rest.
AFTER A FULL DAY OF PARACHUTE JUMPS, THE SKYDIVING INSTRUCTOR HOPED HE WOULD ---

Now arrange the circled letters to form the surprise answer, as suggested by the above cartoon.

Print answer here

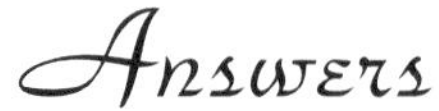

Answers

1. **Jumbles:** OAKEN ABATE PICNIC HOTBED
Answer: Where that stern captain always stood, naturally—AT THE BACK OF THE BOAT

2. **Jumbles:** IRONY ENACT INJURE SHREWD
Answer: That not-so-bright fat guy went to the paint store to get this—"THINNER"

3. **Jumbles:** ABHOR SHINY INVENT PIRACY
Answer: A type of melody evidently requiring considerable effort—"STRAIN"

4. **Jumbles:** CHOKE SWOOP PERMIT TONGUE
Answer: What a man who drinks to forget often forgets—WHEN TO STOP

5. **Jumbles:** CLUCK SCOUT EMPLOY RITUAL
Answer: What they said that snobbish porcupine was—STUCK-UP

6. **Jumbles:** FLUTE SOLAR VERIFY BEYOND
Answer: What a podiatrist does for a living—BILLS THE FOOT

7. **Jumbles:** NEWSY CROON FINALE SOCKET
Answer: When Junior seemed to be spending too much time reading poetry, this is what Dad finally said—"TENNIS, SON?"

8. **Jumbles:** AROMA QUEER BANNER PATTER
Answer: How many times was the "pet menu" revised?—"UMPTEEN"

9. **Jumbles:** SKIMP COWER BARREL DENTAL
Answer: What the bartender who poured those extra big drinks was known as—THE "PLASTERER"

10. **Jumbles:** COLON ENVOY UNPACK TERROR
Answer: A real hothead! Lets you know about goings-on underground—A VOLCANO

11. **Jumbles:** POPPY BYLAW BUNKER GLANCE
Answer: She was looking for a man she could lean on, and ended upgetting one she could do this with—WALK ON

12. **Jumbles:** GOUGE BULGY QUIVER FONDLY
Answer: What the hypochondriac's motto was—GOOD GRIEF

13. **Jumbles:** STEED CHAOS VIRTUE SNUGLY
Answer: What did the snake write at the end of his letter?—LOVE & HISSES

14. **Jumbles:** AMUSE FILMY NEARLY UNTRUE
Answer: What was the down payment on that apartment?—A "FLAT" SUM

15. **Jumbles:** ACUTE PLUME QUARRY SOLACE
Answer: Got a snappy answer when he asked what to do about vermin—"MOUSETRAP"

16. **Jumbles:** GUISE JINGO MEDLEY UNLIKE
Answer: There was plenty of this when a quarrel broke out in the pigpen—MUDSLINGING

17. **Jumbles:** ADAPT CHICK RARELY SCARCE
Answer: "Are they exact copies of the place, sir?"—"REPLICAS"

18. **Jumbles:** TOXIC ASSAY SICKEN UPLIFT
Answer: To get ahead in the oil business, you must be this —"SLICK"

19. **Jumbles:** BUXOM ELUDE RARITY CATCHY
Answer: This is a way-out part of the museum—THE EXIT

20. **Jumbles:** SMOKY ABOVE RATIFY FALTER
Answer: If you break an arm, someone might have to make this for you—THE "BREAK FAST"

21. **Jumbles:** ABYSS CLOVE GADFLY BREACH
Answer: How he knew the clock was wrong—ON THE VERY FACE OF IT

22. **Jumbles:** ESSAY PUPPY FACTOR DINGHY
Answer: This player "botched" his part—"HARPIST"

23. **Jumbles:** TARDY WINCE CHORUS DARING
Answer: How he won that laziness contest—HANDS DOWN

24. **Jumbles:** ENJOY BRAIN FASTEN OUTCRY
Answer: His looks left nothing to be desired—BY ANYONE

25. **Jumbles:** ELOPE GROUP BLOUSE MAGNET
Answer: What those pigs who were close friends must have been—PEN PALS

26. **Jumbles:** GRIPE LIGHT HALVED UNSEAT
Answer: What he said when he fell into the manhole—"GIVE ME A HAND"

27. **Jumbles:** ENEMY WHEAT HYBRID POPLAR
Answer: She always throws away his socks when they're not this—WORTH A DARN

28. **Jumbles:** COMET TRYST BLITHE SYMBOL
Answer: What happened when a couple tried to kiss in a dense fog?—THEY "MIST"

29. **Jumbles:** FLORA AWFUL BAKING DEFAME
Answer: What a man is apt to become when a pretty girl tells him how strong he is—WEAK

30. **Jumbles:** BLAZE RUMMY FORBID MYOPIC
Answer: What poker makes a poor player—POORER

31. **Jumbles:** GUILT EXACT EXEMPT HARROW
Answer: A butcher is a man least likely to put on this—EXTRA WEIGHT

32. **Jumbles:** CRIME HONEY BENIGN AROUSE
Answer: A "shower" for the bride-to-be may symbolize the beginning of this—A "REIGN"

33. **Jumbles:** LOFTY MANLY SCHEME BODICE
Answer: How a shoplifter takes things—AS HE FINDS THEM

34. **Jumbles:** COUGH JUMBO BUCKLE ANYHOW
Answer: What that invisible man definitely was not—MUCH TO LOOK AT

35. **Jumbles:** BASIC HEAVY LAXITY VIABLE
Answer: They strongly felt that the filibusterer should do this—"HALVE" HIS SAY

36. **Jumbles:** MERCY DRONE SPEEDY MOSAIC
Answer: That gossipy dressmaker appeared to know only this about life—THE "SEAMY" SIDE

37. **Jumbles:** WALTZ DRAFT LACING WAYLAY
Answer: Another name for the rush hour—THE CRAWL OF THE WILD

38. **Jumbles:** AGONY FLAME DELUXE WHALER
Answer: The witch ended up here after she did this—FLEW OFF THE HANDLE

39. **Jumbles:** CIVIL ROBIN HYMNAL DINGHY
Answer: He had to work like a horse because his boss was always doing this—"RIDING" HIM

40. **Jumbles:** AZURE CHAFE AFRAID PLAQUE
Answer: What some so-called "dinner parties" sort of are—"LAP-HAZARD"

41. **Jumbles:** UNITY FELON SUCKLE FOSSIL
Answer: What some skiers jump to—"CONTUSIONS"

42. **Jumbles:** ELDER ACAUTE BURIAL DURESS
Answer: It's better to be dead sure at a railroad crossing than this—SURE DEAD

43. **Jumbles:** NEEDY ADAPT CORPSE TRUISM
Answer: That expensive country club has this—MORE DUES THAN DON'TS

44. **Jumbles:** ABYSS TAFFY BANDIT HIDING
Answer: How a boxer makes money—HAND OVER FIST

45. **Jumbles:** TACKY GROUP FIESTA YEOMAN
Answer: What you might see a bouncer throw—A NOISY PARTY

46. **Jumbles:** RODEO ELOPE CATTLE AGENCY
Answer: She likes men with something tender about them, especially when it's this—LEGAL TENDER

47. **Jumbles:** GLADE PLUME DUPLEX ADAGIO
Answer: What the middle-aged Romeo acted like he was—"MUDDLE-AGED"

48. **Jumbles:** BLOOD ICILY CARNAL BEHAVE
Answer: Where the financially embarrassed grave digger usually was—IN A HOLE

49. **Jumbles:** CROON RABBI BEATEN JAGGED
Answer: At thirty a woman is often as old as this—SHE'S GOING TO BE

50. **Jumbles:** RIVET BERET ROBBER WHOLLY
Answer: How a mason learns his trade—BY "TROWEL" & ERROR

51. **Jumbles:** FOIST CHAOS STIGMA UNHOLY
Answer: What the guy who brushed his teeth with gunpowder did—SHOT HIS MOUTH OFF

52. **Jumbles:** FIORD ABATE BEWAIL INJURE
Answer: What they called that nutty ornithologist—"BIRD BRAIN"

53. **Jumbles:** GULCH LAPEL UNRULY BUTANE
Answer: What the guy who was trying to be the life of the party actually managed to be—THE LAUGH OF THE PARTY

54. **Jumbles:** ERUPT BOUND CALLOW AFFIRM
Answer: An enterprising person should not be backward in going there—FORWARD

55. **Jumbles:** ERASE CHIDE HANGER TIDBIT
Answer: What there was in that crowded city—A DEARTH OF EARTH

56. **Jumbles:** FLOOD OCTET EMERGE CUPFUL
Answer: What you might get when the wool is pulled over your eyes—"FLEECED"

57. **Jumbles:** GOURD LOVER BAMBOO REDUCE
Answer: What kind of a husband did she finally marry?—ONE MADE TO "ORDER"

58. **Jumbles:** FLOUT INKED NUANCE RUBBER
Answer: Either a boxer carries out his plans to beat his opponent, or he's this—CARRIED OUT

59. **Jumbles:** ARRAY FUSSY SULTRY RANCOR
Answer: The best way to make up—SAY YOU'RE SORRY

60. **Jumbles:** VYING LIBEL FESTAL CODGER
Answer: As some say, should never get beaten when bad—EGGS

61. **Jumbles:** TEPID SKULK KOWTOW LARYNX
Answer: What the geographer was, naturally—"WORLDLY" WISE

62. **Jumbles:** NOISE ENACT COOPER BROOCH
Answer: In heavy traffic, there's always someone trying to do this—HORN IN

63. **Jumbles:** LEAKY FAIRY BANGLE GROTTO
Answer: What spring should bring after a rough winter—"RE-LEAF"

64. **Jumbles:** SOAPY HURRY BELIEF ELICIT
Answer: What the detectives at that elegant butcher shop were on the lookout for—"CHOP" LIFTERS

65. **Jumbles:** GRIEF DOWDY BIKINI UNLOAD
Answer: Some people consider this an "occupational" disease—WORK

66. **Jumbles:** EVENT BOUGH WEAPON JIGGLE
Answer: What that daring dress she wore at the dance was—MORE GONE THAN GOWN

67. **Jumbles:** BURST TOKEN BANANA ENTITY
Answer: What he said when he was challenged to a duel—"I'LL TAKE A STAB AT IT"

68. **Jumbles:** FABLE CHICK OPAQUE VANITY
Answer: Apparently, a guy who eats and drinks too much would rather be a good liver than this—HAVE ONE

69. **Jumbles:** DIRTY EMPTY FAMILY INTONE
Answer: When a kid fell down while walking through a pasture, it must have been this—A FIELD "TRIP"

70. **Jumbles:** ARMOR POISE BRAZEN JAILED
Answer: This helps many a golfer to improve his score—AN ERASER

71. **Jumbles:** TOPAZ FOCUS OCCULT SNAPPY
Answer: What kind of glasses do foreign agents wear?—"SPY-FOCALS"

72. **Jumbles:** CARGO DOUGH SUGARY REBUKE
Answer: What they said about that crazy entomologist—"HE'S BUGGY"

73. **Jumbles:** CHUTE DAILY EXCISE UNEASY
Answer: What the photogenic mouse knew how to do very well—SAY CHEESE

74. **Jumbles:** BLOAT EXULT ABOUND SAILOR
Answer: What a good pair of handmade shoes should be—BUILT TO "LAST"

75. **Jumbles:** GIVEN DANDY ABRUPT SPONGE
Answer: This kind of running means walking—RUNNING OUT OF GAS

76. **Jumbles:** ALIVE FLUTE MARLIN GALLEY
Answer: The hen crossed over to the middle of the road because she wanted to do this—LAY IT ON THE LINE

77. **Jumbles:** FOAMY JUDGE WHEEZE MATRON
Answer: Where the geology professor brought his students—DOWN TO EARTH

78. **Jumbles:** COLON NOBLE SQUALL TORRID
Answer: A woman goes to a hair stylist when she doesn't want to show this—HER TRUE COLORS

79. **Jumbles:** PLAID MOUSE INNING SAVORY
Answer: What an optometrist is—A MAN OF VISION

80. **Jumbles:** CYCLE PUPIL HAUNCH MAYHEM
Answer: He'll never break his word in a love letter, except with this—A HYPHEN

81. **Jumbles:** TIGER GNOME FEWEST BLUISH
Answer: Every time baby cried they gave him this—THE "WHINE" BOTTLE

82. **Jumbles:** WEIGH FLOUR INBORN BEHELD
Answer: He picked a soft job because he expected to do this later—LIE DOWN ON IT

83. **Jumbles:** SMOKY GAUGE FLAGON PIRACY
Answer: What graduation time was for those young people—THE "PROM" OF LIFE

84. **Jumbles:** GUILE BASIN FLORID EXCITE
Answer: Food some people find edible might seem this to others—INCREDIBLE

85. **Jumbles:** DELVE FLUKE ARMADA PALLID
Answer: What a photographic memory never seems to run out of—FILM

86. **Jumbles:** CROAK SUEDE PANTRY HOTBED
Answer: How an osteopath works his fingers—TO YOUR BONES

87. **Jumbles:** GLORY AUGUR FENNEL PHYSIC
Answer: What a dancer's reputation often rests upon—HER LEGS

88. **Jumbles:** PRONE ONION THRESH INFANT
Answer: What inhibitions do—TIE ONE UP IN "NOTS"

89. **Jumbles:** PAPER GLEAM DARING BLOUSE
Answer: How a pastry chef doesn't live—BY BREAD ALONE

90. **Jumbles:** LYRIC GAUZE CLOVEN FACING
Answer: What you never have if you fall in love with yourself—A RIVAL

91. **Jumbles:** CYNIC PIECE OUTFIT GAMBOL
Answer: What sort of job do they do delivering parcels?—A "BANG-UP" ONE

92. **Jumbles:** LOUSY STAID HEIFER TONGUE
Answer: In Germany, it might provide the answer to the common cold—"GESUNDHEIT"

93. **Jumbles:** CHIME MOOSE DEBATE SURTAX
Answer: What a politician's life often is—A BED OF "RUSES"

94. **Jumbles:** TASTY GRIME SHAKEN ORIGIN
Answer: How a war-monger believes in talking—
WITH HIS ARMS

95. **Jumbles:** GULLY RAINY CARBON POETRY
Answer: Napoleon was the first man who thought he was this—
NAPOLEON

96. **Jumbles:** ERASE AWFUL FLAUNT CODGER
Answer: It's no "feat" to do this—DANCE ON FEET

97. **Jumbles:** GUEST FLAKE BANTER ELICIT
Answer: He drove as if he owned the road which is why he ended up not owning this—A LICENSE

98. **Jumbles:** EXERT FUDGE MYSTIC STOLEN
Answer: What the egotist lets off plenty of—SELF-E"STEEM"

99. **Jumbles:** GROOM PHOTO AGHAST CLOVEN
Answer: What the bubble dancer said when he asked her to marry him—NO SOAP

100. **Jumbles:** AGONY LINER WATERY HOMAGE
Answer: Clothes make the man, especially when worn by this—
THE RIGHT WOMAN

101. **Jumbles:** SWEPT NOISY THIRTY HAPPEN
Answer: After repairs were made on the church spire, it was—
IN TIP-TOP SHAPE

102. **Jumbles:** WHISK DOUBT ACCRUE CHORUS
Answer: When the pianist began the song by playing three notes together, he—STRUCK A CHORD

103. **Jumbles:** VITAL JOIST DEPICT BURGER
Answer: After using a coupon to get the fancy cheese at 70 percent off, they—"SAVER-ED" IT

104. **Jumbles:** NUTTY NINTH DIGEST COSMOS
Answer: He thanked his mime teacher, but was told—
DON'T MENTION IT

105. **Jumbles:** CIVIL COUCH REALLY STEREO
Answer: The churchgoers passed around the offering plate—
COLLECTIVELY

106. **Jumbles:** FLOWN FLAIL CHATTY PIGLET
Answer: They decided to double-up on their mortgage payments, and it was—PAYING OFF

107. **Jumbles:** HUMID DECAY BASKET FRIZZY
Answer: When the owner of the calendar factory gave his employees a big bonus, it—MADE THEIR DAY

108. **Jumbles:** FISHY BLURB BLOTCH TIPTOE
Answer: Drilling through the hard tile would be done—
BIT BY BIT

109. **Jumbles:** FLACK TRACT OUTBID CANNED
Answer: When the squirrel couldn't get the walnut open, his friend wanted—A CRACK AT IT

110. **Jumbles:** DOILY ESSAY RIPPLE PLAGUE
Answer: When he started making fun of his wife's skiing ability, he was on a—SLIPPERY SLOPE

111. **Jumbles:** GOOSE WATCH THEORY BEARER
Answer: When the farmer began selling his own veggies and fruits, the result was a—"GROW-CERY" STORE

112. **Jumbles:** DAZED SLANT LOTION SUMMER
Answer: The twins turning 80 didn't want a party, just the—
SAME OLD, SAME OLD

113. **Jumbles:** LOFTY SWIFT DOUBLE GLOSSY
Answer: She inherited enough to start her business, thanks to her grandmother's—GOOD WILL

114. **Jumbles:** STRUM MOVIE INDUCT SUNKEN
Answer: She picked a book on the history of fat-free milk and—
SKIMMED IT

115. **Jumbles:** DOUGH CATCH UPROAR BUMMER
Answer: When he chose a stage name, Richard Starkey chose one that wasn't—HUMDRUM

116. **Jumbles:** WHEEL CRAZE OUTLET SURVEY
Answer: The twin paramedics were—"TWO" THE RESCUE

117. **Jumbles:** COURT INPUT SWAMPY BUNDLE
Answer: When teaching her students how to chop garlic, the chef didn't—MINCE WORDS

118. **Jumbles:** SHYLY FLING MOSAIC WEIGHT
Answer: It only took about 50 years to go from the Wright Brothers to the 707—TIME WAS FLYING

119. **Jumbles:** PRIOR FOYER INLAND FUMBLE
Answer: When he tried out the barbecue grill his wife got him, he was—FIRED UP

120. **Jumbles:** BURST RISKY LONELY REJECT
Answer: The prison guards approved the new contract and felt that it gave them—JOB SECURITY

121. **Jumbles:** HUMID CHECK MARKET DILUTE
Answer: The magician repaired his faulty prop, and fixing it—
DID THE TRICK

122. **Jumbles:** TOTAL CHORD UNPAID BUSHEL
Answer: It should have been an easy victory for the bocce team, but the player—BOTCHED IT

123. **Jumbles:** GIANT SOUPY SPRAWL BUTANE
Answer: The medieval tailor crated armored outfits for knights. It was his—STRONG SUIT

124. **Jumbles:** POUCH FLINT COSMOS REDUCE
Answer: He needed to pay someone to shovel the melting snow. Luckily, he had a—SLUSH FUND

125. **Jumbles:** SPURN MESSY GARLIC AGENDA
Answer: The church's new choir director was well liked. Members of the choir—SANG HIS PRAISES

126. **Jumbles:** PICKY GROUP MUSSEL MONKEY
Answer: As more telescopes were purchased, the telescope-maker's business was—LOOKING UP

127. **Jumbles:** HONEY BUNNY LOCKET SOCIAL
Answer: The dog who was very good at playing fetch was—
ON THE BALL

128. **Jumbles:** GROWL THIRD FRUGAL FLAVOR
Answer: After eating so much candy, the scary-looking trick-or-treaters were—"FRIGHT-FULL"

129. **Jumbles:** MINUS GOOSE CONCUR DREAMY
Answer: The plant-nursery owners were competitors until they found some—COMMON GROUND

130. **Jumbles:** WAFER YUCKY TRENCH BURROW
Answer: He attached the wires for the EKG quickly. He knew their positions—BY HEART

131. **Jumbles:** BOOTH WOUND FOSSIL VORTEX
Answer: The rescue team reached him in the forest, but he wasn't—OUT OF THE WOODS

132. **Jumbles:** SKIER HELLO LIVING GLOBAL
Answer: The goats that grazed on the slope were—
"HILL-BILLIES"

133. **Jumbles:** PERCH FABLE SPRAIN THRIVE
Answer: To receive her gifts in person, she needed to—
BE PRESENT

134. **Jumbles:** WEARY GOING STEREO PUDDLE
Answer: The competition between the energy companies was a—POWER STRUGGLE

135. **Jumbles:** SINGE FLANK BLOTCH FLAUNT
Answer: He told them that he grew great coffee, but he was—
FULL OF BEANS

136. **Jumbles:** HOUND GLADE MARKET NAPKIN
Answer: After paying to have an amazing deck constructed, the family—HAD IT MADE

137. **Jumbles:** TRACK HATCH NARROW MODULE
Answer: The humans found the aliens to be very sensible and—
DOWN-TO-EARTH

138. Jumble: BLURB WAGER PICKUP PALLET
Answer: When the young players started crying, the baseball field became a—"BAWL" PARK

139. **Jumbles:** DWELL THICK CHANCE MIRROR
Answer: The city was safer because of Dick Tracy's—CRIME WATCH

140. **Jumbles:** PLAZA EMPTY MINGLE ZODIAC
Answer: The little green man from outer space felt alone and—ALIENATED

141. **Jumbles:** GRAND WIPER FEMALE WORTHY
Answer: What's the best way to display a backward drawing?—IN A WINDOW FRAME

142. **Jumbles:** PIVOT PLUME DRENCH PIGLET
Answer: After Ginger gave the kangaroo a coffee, he was—HOPPED UP

143. **Jumbles:** MILKY REBEL ACCRUE CENSUS
Answer: The rookie's dessert was so badly burned, the head chef called it a—"CRIME" BRULEE

144. **Jumbles:** CELLO VISOR FERRET UNWIND
Answer: When Thor invented the wheel, he started a—REVOLUTION

145. **Jumbles:** RIVER GLAZE SKIMPY JESTER
Answer: The hot air balloonists were able to see the sun come up because they were—EARLY RISERS

146. **Jumbles:** ODDLY NIECE SMOKER UPBEAT
Answer: Sherlock Holmes gave his friends discounts, and they were thankful for his—DEDUCTIONS

147. **Jumbles:** STYLE CURVE BALLOT UPROOT
Answer: The mountaintop barbershop was a—CUT ABOVE THE REST

148. **Jumbles:** HANDY MIGHT UNSURE CANOPY
Answer: After rubbing the seasoning on the Thanksgiving turkey, she had—"THYME" ON HER HANDS

149. **Jumbles:** ENACT VIRUS FELLOW CAVORT
Answer: The sea-based wind farm produced this type of energy—"ALL-TURN-ATIVE"

150. **Jumbles:** CANDY SPOIL CUDDLY BELIEF
Answer: The symphony's backup violinist didn't like playing—SECOND FIDDLE

151. **Jumbles:** GROOM FANCY SNEEZE THORNY
Answer: The price of the fancy new recliner was not in his—COMFORT ZONE

152. **Jumbles:** FISHY OPERA TANGLE SPRAIN
Answer: The tips of the darts were dull, so throwing them at the dartboard was—POINTLESS

153. **Jumbles:** TEMPO TWEAK SALMON PICKLE
Answer: When telescopes were invented, people were excited to—TAKE A LOOK-SEE

154. **Jumbles:** RANCH TARDY OPAQUE INVOKE
Answer: When the little boy arrived at the gates of the amusement park, he was—ENTRANCED

155. **Jumbles:** GROUT FUDGE NIMBLE CARAFE
Answer: Teaching rude students to say "thank you" in French class made her—BEG FOR "MERCI"

156. **Jumbles:** OCCUR FUSSY LESSON IMMUNE
Answer: The tractor-trailer driver did OK for himself and was—SEMI-SUCCESSFUL

157. **Jumbles:** ADAPT ABOUT THEORY SCULPT
Answer: When firefighters rescued the kittens from a tree, they averted a—"CAT-ASTROPHE"

158. **Jumbles:** TRULY DITTO BOXING EXTENT
Answer: After they argued about the wrinkled clothes, their problems were—IRONED OUT

159. **Jumbles:** IMAGE CANAL SKINNY HINDER
Answer: After learning that their regular bowling alley was closed, they—CHANGED LANES

160. **Jumbles:** IGLOO THANK TRIPLE CANVAS
Answer: The preparation put into stabbing Dracula in his heart was—PAINSTAKING

161. **Jumbles:** SECOND REFUGE DROWSY ADMIRE UNHOLY BASKET
Answer: What color did he paint the sun and the wind?—THE SUN ROSE, THE WIND BLUE

162. **Jumbles:** MATURE HAWKER AROUND STYMIE NEPHEW PRISON
Answer: How he proposed—IN A MOMENT OF WEAKNESS

163. **Jumbles:** RACIAL ORPHAN INDICT EMERGE PLAGUE FELONY
Answer: What horsemeat is to our dog—FILLY MIGNON

164. **Jumbles:** QUART SALUTE DURESS ACCENT ITALIC SQUALL
Answer: What tears are for many a wife—LIQUID ASSETS

165. **Jumbles:** GIGOLO BICEPS TINKLE LAGOON ANSWER CIPHER
Answer: What they might speak in London's Trafalgar Square—PIGEON ENGLISH

166. **Jumbles:** MARTYR POLICY INFORM BIGAMY UNCOIL ABOUND
Answer: What George Washington made—A DOLLAR GO FAR

167. **Jumbles:** UNWISE POTENT COMEDY AFFIRM SOCIAL FUTURE
Answer: What he said when the judge informed him that he'd been brought before the court for drinking—LET'S GET STARTED

168. **Jumbles:** BROKEN LIZARD FALTER CROTCH IMPAIR PALACE
Answer: They gave the crook a bath so he could do this—"COME CLEAN"

169. **Jumbles:** EMBARK SALOON TUXEDO HINDER LEGACY PHYSIC
Answer: What he was when he found a pearl in the oyster—"SHELL" SHOCKED

170. **Jumbles:** PRISON TRIPLE SALUTE INVOKE MOTIVE ALIGHT
Answer: How to get your clothes off faster than the others—OUTSTRIP THEM

171. **Jumbles:** THEORY SNEEZE SOOTHE IMPEDED GOATEE UNFOLD
Answer: The evening weatherman was worried that the new meteorologist would—STEAL HIS THUNDER

172. **Jumbles:** CURFEW HEALTH STUDIO BUTTON BELLOW SHAGGY
Answer: When Agatha Christie's funeral service was over, they said—THAT'S ALL SHE WROTE

173. **Jumbles:** LAVISH SUNKEN ODDEST CACTUS SURFEY INVOKE
Answer: The retired teacher loved giving the grandkids a—"HIS-STORY" LESSON

174. **Jumbles:** FUSION SOCKET FOURTH DECODE MARKET SICKLY
Answer: She loved the new designer sandals. One pair in particular—KNOCKED HER SOCKS OFF

175. **Jumbles:** HIGHLY INTACT HUMANE TRUDGE GEYSER TYRANT
Answer: She said that her wedding dress still fit, but she was—STRETCHING THE TRUTH

176. **Jumbles:** ASSURE BUDGET FIGURE REVIVE ENROLL NOODLE
Answer: The bodybuilder knew he was in love after experiencing—STRONG FEELINGS

177. **Jumbles:** LIQUID BOUNCE ACCENT GROUND SUDDEN APATHY
Answer: He promised to quit, so when his wife caught him about to smoke a stogie, it was—CLOSE, BUT NO CIGAR

178. **Jumbles:** ONWARD FONDUE PIRACY VISUAL UNIQUE RATHER
Answer: The models walked down the runway in an—ORDERLY FASHION

179. **Jumbles:** TUMBLE TALLER INFORM UNCLOG SCARCE OCCUPY
Answer: When choosing a new yacht, you need to choose the one that—FLOATS YOUR BOAT

180. **Jumbles:** SEESAW OUTAGE PLEDGE PARLOR ELEVEN AFFORD
Answer: After a full day of parachute jumps, the skydiving instructor hoped he would—FALL FAST ASLEEP

Need More Jumbles®?

Order any of these books through your bookseller or call Triumph Books toll-free at 800-335-5323.

Jumble® Books

More than 175 puzzles each!

Cowboy Jumble®
$9.95 • ISBN: 978-1-62937-355-3

Jammin' Jumble®
$9.95 • ISBN: 1-57243-844-4

Java Jumble®
$9.95 • ISBN: 978-1-60078-415-6

Jazzy Jumble®
$9.95 • ISBN: 978-1-57243-962-7

Jet Set Jumble®
$9.95 • ISBN: 978-1-60078-353-1

Joyful Jumble®
$9.95 • ISBN: 978-1-60078-079-0

Juke Joint Jumble®
$9.95 • ISBN: 978-1-60078-295-4

Jumble® Anniversary
$10.95 • ISBN: 987-1-62937-734-6

Jumble® at Work
$9.95 • ISBN: 1-57243-147-4

Jumble® Ballet
$10.95 • ISBN: 978-1-62937-616-5

Jumble® Birthday
$10.95 • ISBN: 978-1-62937-652-3

Jumble® Celebration
$9.95 • ISBN: 978-1-60078-134-6

Jumble® Circus
$9.95 • ISBN: 978-1-60078-739-3

Jumble® Cuisine
$10.95 • ISBN: 978-1-62937-735-3

Jumble® Drag Race
$9.95 • ISBN: 978-1-62937-483-3

Jumble® Explorer
$9.95 • ISBN: 978-1-60078-854-3

Jumble® Explosion
$9.95 • ISBN: 978-1-60078-078-3

Jumble® Fever
$9.95 • ISBN: 1-57243-593-3

Jumble® Fiesta
$9.95 • ISBN: 1-57243-626-3

Jumble® Fun
$9.95 • ISBN: 1-57243-379-5

Jumble® Galaxy
$9.95 • ISBN: 978-1-60078-583-2

Jumble® Garden
$10.95 • ISBN: 978-1-62937-653-0

Jumble® Genius
$9.95 • ISBN: 1-57243-896-7

Jumble® Geography
$10.95 • ISBN: 978-1-62937-615-8

Jumble® Getaway
$9.95 • ISBN: 978-1-60078-547-4

Jumble® Gold
$9.95 • ISBN: 978-1-62937-354-6

Jumble® Grab Bag
$9.95 • ISBN: 1-57243-273-X

Jumble® Gymnastics
$9.95 • ISBN: 978-1-62937-306-5

Jumble® Jackpot
$9.95 • ISBN: 1-57243-897-5

Jumble® Jailbreak
$9.95 • ISBN: 978-1-62937-002-6

Jumble® Jambalaya
$9.95 • ISBN: 978-1-60078-294-7

Jumble® Jamboree
$9.95 • ISBN: 1-57243-696-4

Jumble® Jitterbug
$9.95 • ISBN: 978-1-60078-584-9

Jumble® Journey
$9.95 • ISBN: 978-1-62937-549-6

Jumble® Jubilee
$9.95 • ISBN: 1-57243-231-4

Jumble® Juggernaut
$9.95 • ISBN: 978-1-60078-026-4

Jumble® Junction
$9.95 • ISBN: 1-57243-380-9

Jumble® Jungle
$9.95 • ISBN: 978-1-57243-961-0

Jumble® Kingdom
$9.95 • ISBN: 978-1-62937-079-8

Jumble® Knockout
$9.95 • ISBN: 978-1-62937-078-1

Jumble® Madness
$9.95 • ISBN: 1-892049-24-4

Jumble® Magic
$9.95 • ISBN: 978-1-60078-795-9

Jumble® Marathon
$9.95 • ISBN: 978-1-62937-548-9

Jumble® Parachute
$9.95 • ISBN: 978-1-60078-944-1

Jumble® Safari
$9.95 • ISBN: 978-1-60078-675-4

Jumble® See & Search
$9.95 • ISBN: 1-57243-549-6

Jumble® See & Search 2
$9.95 • ISBN: 1-57243-734-0

Jumble® Sensation
$9.95 • ISBN: 978-1-60078-548-1

Jumble® Surprise
$9.95 • ISBN: 1-57243-320-5

Jumble® Symphony
$9.95 • ISBN: 978-1-62937-131-3

Jumble® Theater
$9.95 • ISBN: 978-1-62937-484-03

Jumble® University
$9.95 • ISBN: 978-1-62937-001-9

Jumble® Vacation
$9.95 • ISBN: 978-1-60078-796-6

Jumble® Wedding
$9.95 • ISBN: 978-1-62937-307-2

Jumble® Workout
$9.95 • ISBN: 978-1-60078-943-4

Jumpin' Jumble®
$9.95 • ISBN: 978-1-60078-027-1

Lunar Jumble®
$9.95 • ISBN: 978-1-60078-853-6

Monster Jumble®
$9.95 • ISBN: 978-1-62937-213-6

Mystic Jumble®
$9.95 • ISBN: 978-1-62937-130-6

Outer Space Jumble®
$9.95 • ISBN: 978-1-60078-416-3

Rainy Day Jumble®
$9.95 • ISBN: 978-1-60078-352-4

Ready, Set, Jumble®
$9.95 • ISBN: 978-1-60078-133-0

Rock 'n' Roll Jumble®
$9.95 • ISBN: 978-1-60078-674-7

Royal Jumble®
$9.95 • ISBN: 978-1-60078-738-6

Sports Jumble®
$9.95 • ISBN: 1-57243-113-X

Summer Fun Jumble®
$9.95 • ISBN: 1-57243-114-8

Touchdown Jumble®
$9.95 • ISBN: 978-1-62937-212-9

Travel Jumble®
$9.95 • ISBN: 1-57243-198-9

TV Jumble®
$9.95 • ISBN: 1-57243-461-9

Oversize Jumble® Books

More than 500 puzzles each!

Generous Jumble®
$19.95 • ISBN: 1-57243-385-X

Giant Jumble®
$19.95 • ISBN: 1-57243-349-3

Gigantic Jumble®
$19.95 • ISBN: 1-57243-426-0

Jumbo Jumble®
$19.95 • ISBN: 1-57243-314-0

The Very Best of Jumble® BrainBusters
$19.95 • ISBN: 1-57243-845-2

Jumble® Crosswords™

More than 175 puzzles each!

More Jumble® Crosswords™
$9.95 • ISBN: 1-57243-386-8

Jumble® Crosswords™ Jackpot
$9.95 • ISBN: 1-57243-615-8

Jumble® Crosswords™ Jamboree
$9.95 • ISBN: 1-57243-787-1

Jumble® BrainBusters™

More than 175 puzzles each!

Jumble® BrainBusters™
$9.95 • ISBN: 1-892049-28-7

Jumble® BrainBusters™ II
$9.95 • ISBN: 1-57243-424-4

Jumble® BrainBusters™ III
$9.95 • ISBN: 1-57243-463-5

Jumble® BrainBusters™ IV
$9.95 • ISBN: 1-57243-489-9

Jumble® BrainBusters™ 5
$9.95 • ISBN: 1-57243-548-8

Jumble® BrainBusters™ Bonanza
$9.95 • ISBN: 1-57243-616-6

Boggle™ BrainBusters™
$9.95 • ISBN: 1-57243-592-5

Boggle™ BrainBusters™ 2
$9.95 • ISBN: 1-57243-788-X

Jumble® BrainBusters™ Junior
$9.95 • ISBN: 1-892049-29-5

Jumble® BrainBusters™ Junior II
$9.95 • ISBN: 1-57243-425-2

Fun in the Sun with Jumble® BrainBusters™
$9.95 • ISBN: 1-57243-733-2